ARCHY LEE

A CALIFORNIA FUGITIVE SLAVE CASE

ARCHY LEE

A CALIFORNIA FUGITIVE SLAVE CASE

RUDOLPH M. LAPP

FOREWORD BY SHIRLEY ANN WILSON MOORE

HEYDAY BOOKS, BERKELEY, CALIFORNIA

BAYTREE BOOKS

This book was made possible in part by a generous grant from the BayTree Fund. Heyday Institute would also like to thank the James Irvine Foundation for their support of Central Valley literature.

First published in 1969 by the Book Club of California.

Library of Congress Cataloging-in-Publication Data

Lapp, Rudolph M.
Archy Lee : a California fugitive slave case / Rudolph M. Lapp ; foreword by Shirley Ann Wilson Moore.
p. cm.
Originally published: San Francisco : Book Club of California, 1969.
ISBN 978-1-59714-080-5 (pbk.)
1. Lee, Archy. 2. Fugitive slaves--California--Biography. 3. Lee, Archy--Trials, litigation, etc. 4. Slaves--Emancipation--United States--Case studies. 5. African Americans--Legal status, laws, etc.--California--History--19th century. 6. California--Race relations--History--19th century. 7. San Francisco (Calif.)--Race relations--History--19th century. 8. Sacramento Valley (Calif.)--Race relations--History--19th century. 9. African American pioneers--California--History--19th century. 10. Frontier and pioneer life--California. I. Title.

E450.L4L3 2008
306.3'62079461--dc22
[B]

2007047363

Cover image and image on p. 25: Mallette Dean. Used by permission of the Estate of Mallette Dean.
Book Design: Lorraine Rath
Photo research and captions: Boyd Williamson
Printing and Binding: Thomson-Shore, Dexter, MI

Orders, inquiries, and correspondence should be addressed to:
Heyday Books
P. O. Box 9145, Berkeley, CA 94709
(510) 549-3564, Fax (510) 549-1889
www.heydaybooks.com

Heyday Books is committed to preserving ancient forests and natural resources. We elected to print *Archy Lee* on 50% post consumer recycled paper, processed chlorine free. As a result, for this printing, we have saved:

5 Trees (40' tall and 6-8" diameter)
2113 Gallons of Wastewater
850 Kilowatt Hours of Electricity
233 Pounds of Solid Waste
458 Pounds of Greenhouse Gases

Heyday Books made this paper choice because our printer, Thomson-Shore, Inc., is a member of Green Press Initiative, a nonprofit program dedicated to supporting authors, publishers, and suppliers in their efforts to reduce their use of fiber obtained from endangered forests.

For more information, visit www.greenpressinitiative.org

Printed in the United States of America

10 9 8 7 6 5 4 3 2 1

CONTENTS

"I WANT IT TO COME OUT RIGHT": RUDOLPH M. LAPP'S *ARCHY LEE: A CALIFORNIA FUGITIVE SLAVE CASE*

Shirley Ann Wilson Moore

Rudolph M. Lapp's publication of *Archy Lee: A California Fugitive Slave Case* in 1969 marked a vital contribution to an emerging field of scholarship devoted to examining the long-overlooked history of African Americans in California and other areas of the West. In the first decades of the twentieth century a small but growing number of historians had begun to challenge the conventional historical wisdom articulated in 1957 by Walter Prescott Webb that the West was a region lacking in "water, timber, cities, industry and Negroes." By the 1940s, however, early scholars of the black western experience were producing works that began to demolish the notion of "black invisibility" in the American saga of western development and settlement.*

One of the best early works on black westerners was Delilah L. Beasley's encyclopedic 1919 book, *The Negro Trail Blazers of California.* Following in Beasley's footsteps, mid-twentieth-century scholars began an outpouring of work detailing the black western experience. As early as 1940 the *Journal of Negro History* published W. Sherman

* For a discussion of black invisibility in the West and for the Walter Prescott Webb quote see: Quintard Taylor, *In Search of the Racial Frontier: African Americans in the American West, 1528–1990* (New York: W. W. Norton and Company, 1988), 19–23.

Savage's "The Negro in the Westward Movement." In 1976 Savage published the groundbreaking book *Blacks in the West.* Similarly, James A. Fisher's exploration of the black western experience in his doctoral dissertation, "A History of the Political and Social Development of the Black Community in California, 1850–1950," expanded the field. Fisher went on to publish other notable works about African American westerners in historical journals during the 1960s and early 1970s. Other important early works of this period include: Eugene Berwanger's *The Frontier against Slavery: Western Anti-Negro Prejudice and the Slavery Extension Controversy*; William Loren Katz's *The Black West*; and Kenneth G. Goode's *California's Black Pioneers: A Brief Historical Survey*.*

In the introduction to the first printing of this painstakingly researched book, Rudolph Lapp noted that "the story of Archy Lee brings together two major themes in American history: the westward movement

* Delilah L. Beasley, *The Negro Trail Blazers of California* (Los Angeles: n.p., 1919; reprint, San Francisco: R and E Research Associates, 1968); W. Sherman Savage, "The Negro in the Westward Movement," *Journal of Negro History* 25 (1940): 533–534, and *Blacks in the West* (Westport, Conn.: Greenwood Press, 1976); James A. Fisher, "A History of the Political and Social Development of the Black Community in California, 1850–1950," Ph.D. dissertation, State University of New York, Stony Brook, 1971. See also, James A. Fisher, "The Struggle for Negro Testimony in California, 1851–1863," *Southern California Quarterly* 51:4 (December 1969), 313–324, and "The Political Development of the Black Community in California, 1850–1950," *California Historical Quarterly* 50:3 (September 1971), 256–266; Eugene Berwanger, *The Frontier against Slavery: Western Anti-Negro Prejudice and the Slavery Extension Controversy* (Urbana: University of Illinois Press, 1967); William Loren Katz, *The Black West* (Garden City, N.Y.: Doubleday and Company, 1971); Kenneth G. Goode, *California's Black Pioneers: A Brief Historical Survey* (Santa Barbara: McNally and Loftin Publishers, 1974); Rudolph M. Lapp, *Blacks in Gold Rush California* (New Haven: Yale University Press, 1977).

and the efforts of black people to achieve full participation in the life of their country."* These two themes are vital to an understanding of the history of African Americans in the West. This book represented a rising tide of black western scholarship that would open the door to a fuller, more complex study of western history and would introduce succeeding generations of students, scholars, and researchers to the African American presence in and influence on the history of the American West.

Archy Lee directs our attention to myriad subjects relative to western history that awaited further exploration: community building, the role of African American women in shaping western history, the dynamics of intra-racial and interracial interaction, multiculturalism, immigration, and the quest for justice and economic equity. These topics also were critical to political, social, and cultural discourse and development in nineteenth-century California. They continue to resonate in the contemporary American western environment.

At first glance, California's Archy Lee case follows the contours of other antebellum fugitive slave cases: in 1858 Archy Lee, a slave, was brought West from Mississippi by his owner, Charles Stovall. Lee asserted his right to liberty on the "free soil" of California. His claim highlighted the clash between property rights and human rights that had beleaguered American courts for more than a century and drew attention to

* Rudolph M. Lapp, *Archy Lee: A California Fugitive Slave Case* (San Francisco: Book Club of California, 1969), v.

the growing national schism over slavery that would eventually lead to the Civil War.

The Archy Lee case was not the first fugitive slave case in the nation, nor was it California's first fugitive slave case since the passage of the state's short-lived Fugitive Slave Act in 1852.* However, Archy Lee's became California's most celebrated fugitive slave case, galvanizing the African American community and revitalizing the abolitionist movement in the state. Indeed, the Archy Lee case has been called California's Dred Scott case, recalling the fateful 1857 Supreme Court decision which proclaimed that blacks, regardless of their status and residence, had no rights in the United States. As compelling as the courtroom drama and legal battles of the case may have been, Rudolph Lapp's book shows that the Archy Lee case was more than just a testament to the vagaries of American antebellum jurisprudence.

The real story lies in what the case tells us about African American agency and their struggle for community and identity in a nation that attempted to deny them these things. It tells us what nineteenth-century African Americans thought of themselves and what they did for themselves. Lapp's research reveals an organized, relatively educated, economically well-positioned, self-confident black population that elected to fight racial barriers by using legal and

* For fugitive slave cases in California preceding the Archy Lee case, see: Shirley Ann Wilson Moore, "'We Feel the Want of Protection': The Politics of Law and Race in California, 1848–1878," in John F. Burns and Richard J. Orsi, eds., *Taming the Elephant: Politics, Government, and Law in Pioneer California* (Berkeley: University of California Press, and San Francisco: California Historical Society, 2003), 109–111.

extralegal means. Their collective power was impressive and often effective.

The book shows the complexity of the western anti-slavery movement and the fight for civil rights. Black supporters of Archy Lee came from all socioeconomic classes and formed the vanguard of an energetic and racially diverse force of abolitionists. This coalition included white men and women whose hostility to slavery mirrored the growing strength of the Republican Party in the nation and around the state. Lapp's book shows how these national political currents were played out within the context of the western experience and how western realities shaped the political debate. When it was first published, this book was a clarion call for further research on western politics in the antebellum era and the role black westerners had in shaping it.

Archy Lee also stands as a critical examination of the quality of western freedom in the nineteenth century. Although California was ostensibly a free state, its constitution and subsequent legislation painfully restricted the lives of African Americans and other people of color. Most antebellum black westerners were newcomers to the state, arriving as freedmen and freedwomen, free people, slaves, and runaways. They made their livings in a variety of ways, including working as miners and sailors, farmers and shopkeepers, business owners and cooks, laundresses and saloon owners, hotel proprietors and blacksmiths, barbers and general laborers. Though they comprised only one percent of the state's total population, their accumulated wealth totaled more than two million dollars. However, California's laws and policies proscribed their aspirations, limiting occupational mobility and barring them from voting, holding public office, giving court testimony against whites, serving on juries, using public transportation, and sending their children to public schools. These conditions made them particularly "well suited to conduct the struggle for full citizenship in their newly adopted home."* It was no coincidence therefore that Archy Lee's most ardent and visible supporters came from the ranks of the black business and entrepreneurial classes. Some, like Mary Ellen Pleasant, San Francisco businesswoman and the "mother of civil rights in California," and Jesse Hackett and Charles Parker, owners of the Hackett House hotel, Sacramento's largest black business and the center of black political activity, were willing to place their livelihoods and lives on the line to harbor and defend the fugitive slave in his bid for freedom.**

Black men and women who were determined to destroy all racial barriers in California forged vibrant communities. In the nineteenth century, however,

* Moore, "'We Feel the Want of Protection,'" 116–117; Clarence Caesar, "The Historical Demographics of Sacramento's Black Community, 1848–1900," *California History,* special edition on African Americans in California (Fall 1996), 204–205.

**For more on the California Colored Conventions, see: Taylor, *In Search of the Racial Frontier*, 90–92. For more on Mary Ellen Pleasant, see: Lynn M. Hudson, "Mining a Mythic Past: The History of Mary Ellen Pleasant," in Quintard Taylor and Shirley Ann Wilson Moore, eds., *African American Women Confront the West, 1600–2000* (Norman: University of Oklahoma Press, 2003), 56–70.

black female activism often was undertaken within a gendered context that rested on a foundation of Victorian notions of female propriety. For example, individual women like Mary Ellen Pleasant and African American women's organizations and church groups were indefatigable fundraisers for and supporters of Archy Lee and other civil rights battles, but organizations like the San Francisco–based Franchise League and the California Colored Convention excluded women from their ranks. Historian Barbara Y. Welke has noted that gender differences have been "implicit yet largely unrecognized in the history of the black civil rights movement in California." The Archy Lee story, like most other early histories of African Americans in the West, represents a starting point for further research into the "gender dimension" that characterized the black western fight for equality and justice. Later generations of scholars and researchers have taken up this challenge, producing works that examine a broad range of African American women's experiences in California and other areas of the West.*

The story of Archy Lee also illustrates the impact of multiculturalism on the black Western experience. The history of African Americans in the West cannot be understood just as a black-white dynamic; African Americans in California also interacted with Chinese, Mexicans, and Indians, living among them and working and socializing with them on a daily basis. Nineteenth-century African Americans and other

* Rudolph M. Lapp, *Archy Lee*, 8.

people of color in the West congregated for mutual aid and protection and at times pooled their resources to fight California's racially restrictive laws. Such laws affected all people of color because, as historian Patricia Limerick has noted, "Western diversity...gave an edge of urgency to each form of prejudice; the line had to be held against each group; if the barrier was breached once, it would collapse before the various 'others.'"* In the four decades that have passed since this book was published, Rudolph Lapp's pioneering inquiry into the Archy Lee case has blossomed into a body of work that is examining broad-ranging themes and topics relative to the nineteenth-century black western experience.** The work of these scholars has

* Barbara Y. Welke, "Rights of Passage: Gendered-Rights Consciousness and the Quest for Freedom, San Francisco, California, 1850–1870," in Taylor and Moore, *African American Women Confront the West,* 74. For a discussion of the "gender dimension" in African American history, see: Darlene Clark Hine, "Black Migration to the Urban Midwest: The Gender Dimension, 1915–1945," in Joe William Trotter, Jr., *The Great Migration in Historical Perspective: New Dimensions of Race, Class, and Gender* (Bloomington: Indiana University Press, 1991) and Evelyn Brooks Higginbotham, "African American Women's History and the Metalanguage of Race," *Signs* 17 (Winter 1992), 251–274. For some recent scholarship dealing with western black women, see: Taylor and Moore, *African American Women Confront the West*; Willi Coleman, "African American Women and Community Development in California, 1848–1900," in Lawrence B. de Graaf, Kevin Mulroy, and Quintard Taylor, eds., *Seeking El Dorado: African Americans in California* (Seattle: University of Washington Press with the Autry Museum of Western Heritage, 2001), 98–125; Shirley Ann Wilson Moore, "Your Life Is Really Not Just Your Own": African American Women in Twentieth Century California," in *Seeking El Dorado*, 210–246.

**Patricia Nelson Limerick, *The Legacy of Conquest: The Unbroken Past of the American West* (New York: W. W. Norton, 1987), 278–279; see also: Moore, "We Feel the Want of Protection," 111–116, and Taylor, *In Search of the Racial Frontier*, 74–77.

expanded our historical knowledge by showing us the impact race, class, and gender have had on the history of the American West. We are all the beneficiaries of Rudolph Lapp's pioneering work.

In 1858 Archy Lee said of his bid for freedom, "I want it to come out right."* We who are historians and students of the black western experience continue to dedicate our efforts to achieving this end as well.

California State University, Sacramento
July 25, 2007

* Some examples of the new western scholarship inspired by Rudolph Lapp and other early scholars of African American history in the West include: Lynn M. Hudson, *The Making of "Mammy Pleasant": A Black Entrepreneur in Nineteenth-Century San Francisco* (Urbana: University of Illinois Press, 2002); Albert S. Broussard, *African-American Odyssey: The Stewarts, 1853–1963* (Lawrence: University of Kansas Press, 1998); Quintard Taylor, *The Forging of a Black Community: Seattle's Central District from 1870 through the Civil Rights Era* (Seattle: University of Washington Press, 1994); Quintard Taylor, *In Search of the Racial Frontier*; Quintard Taylor and Shirley Ann Wilson Moore, eds., *African American Women Confront the West*; Sucheng Chan, Douglas H. Daniels, Mario T. Garcia, Terry P. Wilson, eds., *Peoples of Color in the American West* (Lexington, Mass.: D. C. Heath and Company, 1994); Patricia Nelson Limerick, *The Legacy of Conquest*; Kenneth N. Owens, ed., *Riches for All: The California Gold Rush and the World* (Lincoln: University of Nebraska Press, 2003); and Elizabeth Jameson and Susan Armitage, eds., *Writing the Range: Race, Class, and Culture in the Women's West* (Norman: University of Oklahoma Press, 1997).

INTRODUCTION

By Rudolph M. Lapp

The story of Archy Lee brings together two major themes in American history: the westward movement and the efforts of black people to achieve full participation in the life of their country. It also brings into focus, perhaps for the first time, the degree to which many leading white citizens of California were involved in Negro rights activities in the nineteenth century. Furthermore, Archy Lee's story takes the civil rights activities of California's black men out of the shadows and provides some idea of their scope and vigor.

The first men of African ancestry to join the gold rush in the period of the forty-eighters were sailors from New England. These free black seamen deserted their ships with their fellow whites to rush from San Francisco to the Mother Lode; some of them eventually returned to their homes on the Atlantic seaboard with bags of gold dust.

They were followed within the year by a larger but less fortunate group who came as slaves with their masters as part of the forty-niners. Hundreds arrived, but the actual number who returned with their owners or remained in California as free men is so far unknown.

Black men, free or slave, came to California by all known routes. Most came overland, many came through Panama, a few came by way of the Horn.

In 1850 and 1851 a much larger group of Negroes began to arrive. These were free men. Some sought to find their fortunes in the gold fields, but one may assume that most meant to take advantage of high wages and business opportunities. Like many of their white contemporaries, they viewed California as a temporary stopping place and did not expect to make it their permanent home.

By 1852 there were two thousand black men and women in California. Most were in the cities of San Francisco, Sacramento and Marysville, with smaller pockets in Yuba City and Grass Valley. The Negro population of North American descent in Los Angeles grew more slowly.

Many of these men and women were employed in maritime, culinary and service occupations. For a time it seemed the food service field was almost entirely in black hands. Negro cooks were much in demand in gold rush California. Many Negroes were barbers, and some were clothing merchants. The barbers and stewards and cooks of the inland shipping system served as eyes and ears of the Negro community. After the Mother Lode population waned, some black miners and a few Negroes who took up farming in the upper Sacramento Valley remained. It is possible that the per capita income of California Negroes at this time was higher than that of any comparable group of black men in the United States.

Comprising barely one percent of the total population of California, the Afro-Americans came largely from the big cities of the North Atlantic Coast. Most were from Philadelphia, New York and the cities of New England, but they also included persons from the free Negro communities of the slave states of Maryland and Virginia. Before the Civil War, an undetermined number of slaves entered the California Negro community by achieving freedom one way or another while in California. Some of them effected successful escapes and others, often by prearrangement, were given freedom papers by their masters. These arrangements were recorded by local governments and copies of these freedom papers can still be seen in the archives of the Mother Lode counties.

Not long after arrival the black population began to build its own community organizations. By 1852 the first Negro church was open in San Francisco. Before the Civil War, religious needs of black people in Northern California were ministered to by black preachers in Sacramento, Stockton and Marysville. During this period, self-help and fraternal groups were also organized.

The Franchise League, the first civil rights group, was organized by San Francisco Negroes in 1852. At this early date the black population had accumulated enough property to feel the need to protect it by democratically dispensed justice. The new state, by not allowing Negro testimony to be presented on an equal basis with white testimony in court cases, failed to provide judicial democracy. In the courts of California the word of a well-educated and respected black man did not carry the weight of the word of a white scoundrel. This inequity robbed Negroes of legal defense in cases where there was no white witness. The Franchise League was organized to mobilize white public opinion to change the state law so that testimony from whites and blacks would be treated equally. While a great deal of white support was rallied for this campaign—especially from the San Francisco community—these efforts failed.

The work of the San Francisco–based Franchise League was broadened by the call for the first California Colored Convention in Sacramento in 1855. The black population was still growing, and stable communities could be found in Sacramento, Stockton and Marysville, as well as in scattered locations throughout the Mother Lode. A statewide executive committee was formed to continue the attempt to amend the law about testimony. This work went on during successive conventions in 1856 and 1857. Thousands of white signatures were obtained in petition campaigns, but the law was not changed. Announcement of the Dred Scott Decision of the United States Supreme Court in 1857 further lowered the morale of the California Colored Convention that year.

Despite the frustrations of the testimony fight (which did not succeed until 1863), the Negro community continued to prosper and its institutions to become more stable. Many leaders of the convention movement were well-to-do businessmen. Negro churches increased in size and number throughout

California. Black men experienced in journalism even founded in 1855 a Negro weekly newspaper, the *Mirror of the Times*, but after several dozen numbers it passed out of existence some time in 1857. Only two issues are extant.

Black children had had to rely on their churches for elementary education until, after much pleading with educational authorities, in the 1850s the California Negro leaders finally persuaded school authorities—first in San Francisco and then Sacramento—to provide schools for black children. These were segregated until after the end of the Civil War.

Such was the situation of the Negro in California at the time that Archy Lee was arrested. His was by no means the first fugitive slave case in gold rush California. As early as 1850 there were black men who decided to make a strike for freedom. Some attempts succeeded; others failed. A man's luck usually depended on the kind of judge he faced when his freedom became a court case. California law in the early fifties was so irregular that the special prejudices of each judge were the deciding factor.

The fortunate black man was one who found himself facing a judge of New England or upstate New York antecedents. In these instances the judge usually referred to the California constitution and earlier Mexican law and ordered the Negro freed. But many black men were remanded to their masters and sent back to slavery. In the case of Stephen Hill of Gold Springs, Tuolumne County, when the court ordered him back into slavery, white friends spirited him out of jail, and one slaveowner never saw his alleged property again. But this kind of thing did not happen frequently.

By the time the Archy Lee case became a celebrated issue in California, fugitive slave cases were rare. Most slaveowners in the East were well aware that California intended to remain a free state. A state fugitive slave law had been allowed to lapse by 1855. It is true that the state legislature was dominated by Democrats, but many of them were free-soilers. Antislavery societies did not exist in California, but there was the Colored Convention movement.

While there were no white antislavery organizations in California, there were individual whites in the state who were hostile to slavery. Some were in the legal profession and willing to face unfriendly public opinion for their beliefs. Most of the men who defended Archy became highly respected figures in the history of the state and were associated with the young Republican party of California.

Most of the names mentioned in the following text are those of the white men on both sides of this celebrated case because contemporary accounts give little information about the black men who were involved. A mature journalism would have investigated the leadership of the Colored Convention movement, for its members were the ones who sought out lawyers and raised monies to pay the costs of this expensive legal battle. These little-known black men included persons of better-than-average education with great qualities of leadership. Many had been leaders in the Negro communities of Philadelphia, New York, Boston and New Bedford. They had worked closely with Frederick Douglass and William Lloyd Garrison in the antislavery movement; many had worked with the Underground Railroad. Some had been educated at Oberlin College. In a racially democratic society, many would have been national leaders.

Sources for this story were primarily the San Francisco and Sacramento newspapers. Added material was found in the white and black antislavery press in the East. The histories of California by Bancroft and Hittell make useful, though brief, references to the case. Oscar Shuck's book on the bench and bar in California has material about most of the lawyers involved but makes only one reference in its 1,152 pages to the Archy Lee case.

Thanks must be given to the following for their advice and counsel: Robert Becker and the gracious staff of the Bancroft Library, U.C. Berkeley, Professor Kenneth M. Stampp, Ruth and Herman Schein of Parnassus Press, and my wife, Patricia T. Lapp, whose assistance was invaluable. A portion of the research on Archy was accomplished with the assistance of a grant from the American Philosophical Society.

ARCHY LEE

A CALIFORNIA FUGITIVE SLAVE CASE

ONE

On Wednesday night, January 6, 1858, police went to Hackett House—a rooming house run by local Negroes at Third between K and L streets in Sacramento, California—to arrest a young Mississippi-born black named Archy Lee. Lee was in hiding there because he had learned a few days before that Charles Stovall, with whom he had come across the plains to California several months earlier, was planning to take him back to the Stovall family plantation in Mississippi.

Although he might have been unclear about his status when he came to California, Archy knew he would return to the South as a slave. Perhaps the thought of the many miles between Mississippi and Sacramento helped give him courage to take his first big step toward freedom.

Soon after his arrival in California, Archy Lee had learned that slavery was illegal there. He also discovered that California Negroes, organized in the Colored Convention movement, were experienced in helping black men to gain their freedom after they had been brought as slaves to the state. This group was sizeable in Sacramento, and during the months that Archy worked in various jobs around that city he had met several convention members. Some of these new friends probably lived at Hackett House, since it was there he went to hide after his momentous decision to escape from his former master.

In a southern city before the Civil War, Archy's story would have ended with his arrest that January night. In Sacramento, however, the statewide Colored Convention was not only strong, but it also had influential friends among white citizens. These forces combined swiftly to defend Archy.

In less than twenty-four hours, Charles Parker, one of the Negro owners of Hackett House, had a writ of habeas corpus drawn up to free Archy from the city prison on the grounds that he was being illegally detained. White lawyers drew up the writ; there were no Negro lawyers in California. California was not unique, for in the United States of 1858 there were virtually no opportunities for Negroes to get legal training, and the few blacks who could practice law lived in the New England states.

Thursday morning, January 7, County Judge Robert Robinson had the writ in his hands. At Charles Parker's side were the prominent Sacramento attorneys Edwin B. Crocker and John H. McKune, whose offices were in the Read Block on Third and J streets, barely two blocks from Hackett House. Parker, however, had gone to Crocker's office for reasons other than proximity. He went because Edwin Bryant Crocker, brother of Charles Crocker, subsequently famous as one of the Big Four of the Southern Pacific Railroad, was himself already well known as a liberal lawyer. Some years before he had worked with another Sacramento attorney, Cornelius Cole, in behalf of fugitive slaves. Crocker's hostility to slavery had begun before he came to California. In 1844 he had voted for the antislavery Liberty party, becoming a member of its national committee eight years later. In the early 1850s as a young lawyer in Indiana he had defended a fugitive slave.

Judge Robinson called a hearing for the next afternoon. That January 8 was also historically interesting because it was the day when John B. Weller, a pro-southern man, was inaugurated in Sacramento as fifth governor of the state of California. The new legislature, overwhelmingly Democratic, was also extremely hostile to the aspirations of black people.

In the courtroom the number of spectators, although not large, contained a high percentage of Negroes, according to the newspapers. The son of a Mississippi plantation owner, Charles Stovall was determined not to lose Archy. Not only had he come to depend on him, but Archy was worth $1,500 in the slave state of Mississippi. Stovall's attorney, James H. Hardy, was a strong proslavery man who later, as a judge during the Civil War, was impeached by the California legislature for cheering the Confederate cause.

Judge Robinson faced the contending arguments. Archy's lawyers maintained that the laws of California made Archy a free man. Crocker concluded that

Archy was not a fugitive slave because he had not run away from Mississippi. Since it was agreed that Archy had separated himself from Stovall in the free state of California, Archy was therefore being held illegally in the Sacramento jail.

Stovall's lawyers maintained that Archy was a slave according to Mississippi law, and, since Mississippi should be respected, therefore he was still Stovall's slave. The legal arguments and their specialized jargon were little understood by Archy, though he listened intently to the proceedings, his concern and courage mingled with confusion and fear. Stovall's lawyers claimed that since Archy did not himself ask for a writ to gain his freedom, he might not be interested in it.

Judge Robinson took a moment to ask Archy if he really were interested in being set free. Perhaps feeling that no answer was better than a fatally wrong one, Archy remained silent. His untrained judgment was probably sound. As events progressed, however, he gained courage and a sense of timing and came to express himself clearly in his own words.

Realizing that Judge Robinson was not going to act swiftly to return Archy to slavery, Stovall's lawyers took a new approach. They decided to involve United States Commissioner George Pen Johnston, a southerner by birth, who was in Sacramento from San Francisco, probably to attend Governor Weller's inauguration.

Stovall's lawyers maintained that because Archy owed service in another state, Johnston had the power to rule that he be taken back to Mississippi without interference from California. Johnston was not sure the case came under his jurisdiction. He left to spend several days in San Francisco in private discussions with experienced legal talent. Press reports suggested he was in conference with the famous Judge Hall McAllister, who had come to California from Georgia and who still supported slavery.

Commissioner Johnston received the case on Saturday, January 9, and made his decision four days later. Meanwhile, Archy was in the Sacramento jail. Neither the Stovall forces nor Archy's friends proposed he be released on bail during this period. Each side had its own reasons for wanting him confined.

Johnston finally decided that he did not have jurisdiction in the case. Archy had not crossed state lines in running away from Stovall but had made his strike for freedom *within* the boundaries of the state of California. Johnston may have thought he had successfully disengaged himself from an awkward case. He was mistaken. He became even more deeply involved later on.

TWO

The Johnston decision returned the case to the state courts. On Saturday, January 23, Judge Robinson once more took it up and once again Hardy represented Stovall. But this time Archy's attorney was a new and distinguished member of the Sacramento legal community, Joseph W. Winans. Winans, who had his offices in the same building as Crocker and McKune, had also been involved previously in fugitive slave cases on the side of the Negro. In later years he earned a reputation as the most scholarly member of the California Bar.

Statewide interest in the case had developed. As Archy was brought from jail, the court chamber was filled, many of those present being Negroes. At the start of the proceedings Hardy repeated the claim that Archy had had nothing to do with the matter of his freedom and that, in effect, *outsiders* were responsible for the whole affair. As he had done previously, Judge Robinson turned to Archy and asked if he wished to remain in California or return to Mississippi. This time, to the relief of his black brothers in the audience, Archy did not remain silent. He replied,

"I don't understand what you are speaking of, but I want it to come out right. I *don't* want to go back to Mississippi."

The subsequent three hours were occupied with witnesses presenting their statements and Winans and Hardy arguing their respective cases. Information about the lives of Archy and Stovall before their arrival in California was brought out, and it was learned that during the summer of 1857 Charles Stovall decided to travel from Mississippi to California to improve his health. His voyage began in Carroll County, where his family had a plantation and Archy Lee had been a slave. Stovall and Archy had crossed the plains together, but the evidence was not clear as to where they met to start the journey. One version said the two of them left Mississippi together. Another claimed that Stovall met Archy in Missouri.

According to the latter story, they met there because Stovall wanted to take Archy west but had to let him flee from Mississippi when Archy wounded a white man in a fight there. According to this story Stovall started off alone on his journey, picked up Archy in Missouri, and together they headed across the plains to California. The pair drove a herd of cattle which they left in Carson Valley, where Stovall bought a ranch. They arrived in Sacramento in October 1857.

Stovall stated he planned only a temporary stay in California—eighteen months at most. This claim was important because much of the case rested on whether

Stovall's residence in California was that of permanent resident or traveler. The California constitution protected travelers in their possession of slaves but, to prevent slavery from taking root in the state, it did not permit permanent residents to own slaves.

Short of funds when he arrived in Sacramento, Stovall hired out Archy for wages and took a portion of them. Then he opened a private school in which he taught for two months. These were not practices of a "traveler," as Archy's attorneys were swift to point out.

The evidence suggests that Stovall was not a harsh master. Rather he was an unrealistic young man, unaware or contemptuous of the status of Negroes in California. Either he failed to have much respect for the California constitution or simply did not read it on matters concerning slavery. He might have read newspapers on occasion and discovered that the three or four thousand Negroes living in California in 1857 were represented by their own civil rights and church organizations. He might have known that by the end of that year they had had their third Colored Convention. After several months' residence in Sacramento it is likely that he realized the presence of large numbers of free Negroes would begin to have an effect on Archy. Perhaps on the advice of fellow southerners he decided in the first days of January 1858 to send Archy back to Mississippi before it was too late. But it was already too late. The advice of the free Negroes had worked faster.

When all the evidence had been presented and the lawyers' presentations completed, Judge Robinson stated he would hand down a decision on the following Tuesday, January 26. Before the litigants left the court and Archy was returned to the Sacramento prison, it became evident that Stovall's attorneys were reaching for a new approach for their client. They were considering taking the case out of Judge Robinson's court to the State Supreme Court. While Archy's lawyers were dubious about this development, they saw some merit in it as a way of making the state constitution's meaning clear on the matter of taking slaves to California. Winans was certain the definition of a "traveler" was so clear and Stovall fitted the definition so badly that Archy was sure to be given his freedom. Perhaps Hardy rested his hopes for returning Archy to slavery on the fact that in 1858 southerners outnumbered northerners two to one in California's highest court, and all the justices were Democrats.

On the afternoon of Tuesday, January 26, Archy was brought back to Judge Robinson's court. At three o'clock the judge handed down his decision. Archy was to go free. The words were hardly said when he was rearrested. This occurred because Stovall's lawyers had communicated with Justice David Terry of the State Supreme Court, and he had agreed to use his special powers to issue a writ requiring that the case be brought before the justices of his court. With this in their hands, Stovall's attorneys were able to get a warrant to rearrest Archy. It is hard to believe that Judge Robinson had no inkling of what was to happen. When Archy became a prisoner again the many spectators were stunned. Half of them were Negro, and they walked with Archy as he was being led back to jail.

At this time the State Supreme Court was composed of three men: Chief Justice David Terry and Associate Justices Peter H. Burnett and Stephen J. Field. Although all were Democrats, Terry and Burnett were southerners and decidedly hostile to Negro freedom, while Field was Connecticut-born with moderate antislavery views. Before coming to California Peter Burnett had been in politics in Oregon, where he was instrumental in putting anti-Negro laws into the state constitution. He was particularly hostile to immigration of free Negroes to the West.

For Archy this new development meant confinement for more than two additional weeks in the Sacramento city prison. The emotional strain upon him must have been intense, but his Negro and white friends were probably in contact with him through these weeks to give him moral strength. They certainly were not idle. The movement to free Archy had spread from Sacramento, with its three to four hundred blacks, to San Francisco, where the Negro community was much larger and better organized. There were nearly one thousand Negroes in San Francisco in 1858.

At eleven o'clock on Friday, February 5, a small group of men came together to decide Archy's fate. Unfortunately, little is known of the informal elements of this confrontation between two justices of the State Supreme Court and the lawyers for Archy and Stovall, although we do know that Justice Field was ill and not present.

The newspapers reported that attorneys Winans and Hardy took one hour and a half each to make their presentations. Flaring tempers or unreported asides were never noted in the recollections of the participants in the years that followed this historic event nor in the unemotional record of this decision printed in twenty-four pages of the 1858 California Reports. The justices announced that they would render a decision the following Thursday.

In late afternoon on February 11, the court met to make public its decision. The opinion had been written by Justice Burnett, but it was Terry who notified those present. He simply announced that the court judged that Archy should be given back to Stovall.

The scene that followed was one of angry confusion. Archy was immediately escorted back to the police station by several policemen. The large crowd—divided between supporters of Archy and Stovall—followed. Archy himself was desperate. Three times he attempted to escape on the route between the court and the station house. There were probably as many people who wanted to help him as there were those who joined Stovall to prevent such action. Archy Lee was soon in prison again.

THREE

Justice Burnett's written opinion shocked many lawyers and journalists alike. On all major points Burnett agreed that Stovall did not fit the definition of a traveler. But, claimed the justice, since Stovall was such a young and inexperienced man, and since this was the first time that the court had faced such a case, the court could show kindness and give Archy back to Stovall and slavery!

The press described the decision as everything from "lame and impotent" to a "crowning absurdity." Some wanted to see Terry and Burnett impeached. The feeling was widespread that these two men had surrendered the dignity of the State Supreme Court to appease prejudice.

The *Alta California* maintained that California now stood disgraced in the eyes of the nation, and only the removal of Terry and Burnett could clear its name. A wit who signed himself "Justicia" wrote the *Alta* from Rattlesnake Bar in Placer County to submit his satirical "syllabus" for California lawyers based on this decision. Some of his guidelines were:

> The Constitution never operates for the first time.
>
> The Constitution never operates against a man travelling for his health.
>
> Charity is defined, "to take a man away from himself and give him to another."
>
> A man may gain all the law in his case but lose himself.

The satirist was later revealed to be Joseph Glover Baldwin, author of the popular humorous book *The Flush Times of Alabama and Mississippi*, who himself would soon become a member of the California Supreme Court.

Supreme Court decisions usually carry a quality of finality, but this proved far from true in this case. The usually moderate *San Joaquin Republican*, a Stockton paper that reflected the views of those California Democrats who were trying to avoid the controversial slavery issue, said that the facts showed that by law Stovall should have lost the slave. "Then the order of rendition of the boy is void and the question left just where it was."

The *Sacramento Daily Union* conjectured further:

> But suppose the slave Archy is again brought before a District or County Judge upon a writ of Habeas Corpus; would not the judge be fully authorized to discharge him upon the law as laid down by the Supreme Court?

The case touched the lives of many in California. At that time there was economic depression in both state and nation. The Chinese, more numerous in California than Negroes, were serious competitors for the limited number of jobs. With this situation as background, the state legislature, reflecting the Democratic victory in 1858, was not only anti-Negro but also anti-Chinese. The young, antislavery Republican party, though led by some of the ablest men in California, was small.

There was talk early in the year of limiting non-white immigration into the state. Archy's case probably triggered the presentation of a bill designed to prevent further free Negro immigration to California. (One supporter of the bill in effect said this on the floor of the state assembly. His anti-Negro prejudices were offended by the militancy with which the California colored community rallied to Archy's defense.) The majority of the Democrat-dominated legislature favored it; only an accident of timing prevented the bill from becoming law in April 1858. If the threat of such legislation was meant to frighten the Colored Convention movement, it failed to do so in matters concerning Archy Lee.

The heat generated by Archy's case so increased the general anti-Negro prejudices that one black man, wholly unrelated to the trial, was killed, probably as an indirect result of it. This was Aaron Bracy, a Negro farmer in the mining community of Auburn, known as a man of independent spirit and hot temper. In February Bracy sold part of his land to a white man named Barney Murphy. Somewhere in the course of the negotiations an argument developed, and Bracy plunged a pick into Murphy's head. Bracy himself went to the authorities to report the affair. He brought them back to the still-living Murphy so that he could get medical aid and then surrendered himself to await trial. But the white people of Auburn wanted blood and had a special hate for Bracy. They lynched him while Murphy was still alive. Local officials and a Catholic priest pleaded to no avail against this illegal and horrible act. The press viewed the Auburn mob's behavior with disgust.

FOUR

For some weeks after the Supreme Court decision, Archy's whereabouts was a Northern California mystery and guessing game. Within forty-eight hours Archy had been taken from the Sacramento prison in irons, Stovall and a guard accompanying him, in an open, two-horse carriage. Since that time his destination had been unknown. There were reports that not only was Archy in chains, but that his escorts were well armed.

Rumors about Archy and his destination varied widely. Some had him headed back to Carson Valley. Others claimed he was on a steamer sailing for the Pacific en route to Mississippi.

One placed him on a Wells Fargo stagecoach headed east, with Stovall holding a receipt for him to the value of $2,000 in case he escaped. This was especially unrealistic. Wells Fargo would have been foolhardy to take on such business even if the firm might not have heard of the Illinois case in which a southerner sued a railroad company for the value of his slave because the slave had used the moving train to effect an escape.

The rumor that proved true was that Archy was in Stockton. On February 21 a Stockton newspaper noted that "Archy came to this city a few days ago." This bland comment was given dramatic detail when a letter signed "Hand-Cuff" appeared in a San Francisco newspaper. The writer said:

> I know where Archy is. He is in the Stockton jail—put there for "safekeeping"...I have seen him every other day since he has been there. The jail is a gloomy little building, on the banks of the slough, adjacent to the courthouse; from the flagstaff off which floats "the star spangled banner." Long may it wave o'er the land of the free and the home of the slave.

However, apparently Archy was not without friends in Stockton. It was a town which had its own small Negro community; and it had been founded by Captain Charles M. Weber, an antislavery German immigrant.

Stockton was to be Archy's "place of residence" for more than two weeks, during which his fate was still the subject of conjecture. Rumor had it that he would be secreted aboard some vessel in San Francisco Bay, an event that would not take place without an attempt by rescuers to kidnap him. These speculations gained strength as Negro patrols were noted on the wharves of San Francisco. They seemed to be on scheduled shifts. During the first days of March the organized Negro community watched intently. Unsympathetic jokesters taunted tense black patrols by yelling alarms that cabs, actually decoys, were rushing away with Archy.

In the belief that he might come into San Francisco by boat, Negro patrols watched with particular anxiety when word reached them that the Stockton steamer was due. It was reported that at times these groups ranged from fifty to one hundred and fifty persons. They were so apprehensive of some secret Stovall maneuver that when a skiff went from one wharf to another, they raced to make sure that Archy was not being moved secretly. The excitement brought many onlookers down to the wharves.

On the morning of Friday, March 5, the waterfront crowds grew in size and fervor with rumors that Archy was in or near San Francisco. Two ships in port were near sailing time. The *Golden Age* was at the Market Street wharf, and the *Orizaba* was scheduled to sail for Panama that day. At eleven o'clock a rumor spread that Archy was hidden at North Beach or Alcatraz and would be spirited onto one of the steamers as it passed. As the *Alta California* put it: "Two boats were manned with stalwart blacks, determined to make a last effort to rescue their fellow from a return to slavery." Archy, however, was not there; at noon his whereabouts was still not known.

Judging from the welter of reports and rumors, the following is roughly what happened to Archy after he left Stockton. On Monday, March 1, Stovall and Archy departed from the Stockton city jail and approached San Francisco in slow stages, remaining for half a day in some places along the route. One report had them passing through San Jose. Stovall may have thought he was being clever with this approach to his problem. Perhaps his accomplices in the Bay Area suggested this style of travel. They had learned that the organized Negroes, having discovered Archy in Stockton, were on the verge of obtaining a writ to free him there. To avoid this, Stovall was forced to leave the city and wander about before meeting his boat in San Francisco. Evidently his objective was Oakland; from there he hoped to spirit Archy aboard the *Orizaba*. Obviously Stovall did not yet feel secure in possession of his "slave." They spent Thursday night somewhere in Oakland.

Unknown to himself, Stovall may have been under constant surveillance from the moment he left Stockton. While California, unlike Massachusetts, had no semblance of an organized abolitionist movement, it did have an organized free Negro movement that more than made up for the lack. It drew its main strength from San Francisco but spread throughout California, whose total Negro population was close to four thousand in 1858.

Just as in Sacramento, the Negro Convention movement in San Francisco had many individual white friends who sympathized with its aspirations. But the heart of the resistance to Archy's re-enslavement was in the strong activist group of black Californians. All classes of Negroes were involved. During this crisis Negro businessmen closed their offices to man the wharves alongside maritime workers. This last group was most important because many Negro leaders worked as stewards, cooks, waiters, and deckhands on ships that plied the waters of the bay, and like the Negro barbers, they were the eyes and ears of the Negro organization.

The intensity of feeling in the San Francisco Negro community over this issue led many whites to believe that an illegal rescue was being planned. This was not so. While Archy and Stovall were still in Oakland, San Francisco Negroes schemed to free Archy by legal means. All of the hurried, frenzied behavior along the bay was part of a plan which first involved obtaining a writ of habeas corpus to take Archy out of Stovall's hands, and next the making of a complaint charging Stovall with kidnapping in order to have him arrested.

James Riker, a steward and a leader among San Francisco Negroes, signed both the complaint and the writ. The writ for Archy was issued by County Judge T. W. Freelon; the warrant to arrest Stovall for kidnapping came from Justice Austin's office. Both legal documents were given to a San Francisco deputy sheriff and two of his officers. On March 5 these three men were as much in evidence on the wharves of San Francisco as the Negro patrols. The latter kept in close touch with these officers; it was their intent to hail them should they glimpse Archy or Stovall before the officers did.

When the *Orizaba* prepared to lift anchor at the Vallejo Street wharf shortly after noon, Archy's whereabouts was still unknown. All through the night

Negro patrols had been watching the *Orizaba* as well as other ships. With the coming of morning the officers, who had also been up all night, separated to take up posts near the *Golden Age* and the *Orizaba*. Crowds at the wharf included many curiosity seekers as well as partisans of both Stovall and Archy. The noisiest were Stovall's supporters, who cheered and joked as the *Orizaba* pulled away into the bay, but her passengers also yelled from sheer excitement.

In the confusion hardly anyone noticed that the deputy sheriff and his two officers had quietly boarded the *Orizaba*. These local lawmen may have heard rumors that an attempt would be made to put Archy and Stovall aboard the ship in the middle of San Francisco Bay. (According to Helen Holdredge, the biographer of Mammy Pleasant, whose husband at this time was cook on the *Orizaba*, the ship's owners had antislavery sympathies. It is possible, therefore, that the sheriff was acting on more than guesswork when he suspected that a midday boarding would take place.)

As the ship moved slowly toward the Golden Gate, the three men scanned the bay and also watched closely for any evidence that some of the passengers were in collusion with Stovall. When Officer Lees saw one wave a handkerchief in the direction of Angel Island, he was instantly alert. Another handkerchief waved in reply from a rowboat close to Angel Island. Soon this boat drew alongside the *Orizaba*. Four men were visible. From descriptions they had been given, the officers recognized Stovall, but not until the rowboat was alongside the ship was Archy seen. He had been compelled to crouch in the bottom to stay out of view.

Just as Stovall was about to board the *Orizaba,* a passenger, recognizing one of the officers, yelled to him: "Keep off, keep off! There are officers aboard!" But Officer Lees, his heart in his work, leaped into the rowboat—at the risk of going through the bottom—and seized Archy. Pro-Stovall passengers tried to stop the officers but failed. Lees picked up Archy, who was small, and handed him to the other officers on deck. Stovall and the men from the rowboat boarded and a short period of bedlam ensued. Threats of resistance were made as Lees served his warrant on Stovall. Some of the passengers took sides. But the ship's officers and most of the passengers favored obeying the law. The threats were never carried out.

One old lady, described as wearing "spectacles and extensive crinoline," rushed in to help Archy shouting, "You varmints! We'll see whether free people are to be kidnapped in this way!" An old Negro on board shouted "Hosanna!" as Archy entered the police boat tied to the *Orizaba.* Still, not all comment was friendly. One passenger yelled, "Kill the damned nigger thief!"

FIVE

Archy now entered a new phase in his struggle for freedom. Crouching in the rowboat headed for the *Orizaba*, he must have felt that each dipping of the oars took him farther from freedom. Presumably he knew nothing of the plans to rescue him, for there is no hint that Archy had had any contact with friends during the five days it had taken Stovall to bring him from Stockton to Oakland. As the rowboat pulled away on signal from Angel Island towards the *Orizaba*, the waters of the bay probably gave Archy a feeling of isolation and helplessness. He must have been astonished and then numbly surprised when he heard the shouting and saw Officer Lees leap into the boat. He understood the meaning of Lees's action, for he showed no resistance when the officer lifted him bodily and placed him on the ship. Contemporary accounts say he watched everything intently but said nothing. Only one newspaper reported any comment. Somewhere between the wharf and the San Francisco courtroom, he was alleged to have remarked that there was no need for him to say anything because "white folks was doing enough talking for everybody!"

Archy was rowed to shore in the police boat that the officers had attached to the *Orizaba* for that purpose. An immense crowd on shore greeted them with cheers. Archy was, as many of the newspapers called him, "the observed of all observers." The crowd grew as he and the three officers proceeded up the street towards the sheriff's office. The Negro residents of San Francisco were out in full force and highly elated. As the *San Francisco Chronicle* reported the following day: "The colored population of the town were considerably excited, thronging the City Hall in large numbers, yet perfectly orderly in their conduct."

That same Friday afternoon Archy was brought to Judge Freelon's court, where he was taken in custody officially and then sent to the county jail to await an official hearing the following Monday morning. In another court Stovall paid $500 in bail to keep himself out of jail until his hearing came up the following day.

Later that afternoon signs began to appear in public places in the Negro community announcing a meeting at eight o'clock that night in the Zion African Methodist Episcopal Church located on Pacific Street just above Stockton. This congregation, organized by the Reverend J. J. Moore in 1852, was one of the first Negro churches in San Francisco, and with Moore still its pastor, it was an integral part of Negro rights activities. By seven-thirty that evening there was an overflow crowd, including a number of white persons, in the church. When the meeting began, the first order of business was a call for a fundraising campaign for the expenses of Archy's case. A committee of seven men and seven women was appointed. Next came speeches by some of the outstanding leaders of the Colored Convention movement. The Reverend J. J. Moore addressed the assemblage, as did Mifflin Wistar Gibbs, who became a federal judge in Little Rock, Arkansas, after the Civil War. They said that the Negro community of San Francisco should maintain its exemplary behavior and not commit any overt acts that might alienate white friends from Archy's cause. At the end of the meeting a collection of $150 was taken.

Raising funds was a pressing problem. Although white lawyers in New England frequently refused to accept fees in fugitive slave cases, this did not seem to be true in California. The entire California Negro community was called upon to support the drive, and George Washington Dennis was but one of several black businessmen who went into debt to help pay Archy's legal fees. A year later Negro churches were holding benefits to raise funds to repay Dennis. Whites were also asked to make contributions, through advertisements in the *California Daily Chronicle*.

It has not been recorded that financial assistance was sent from the antislavery centers on the East Coast, but it is known that they were aware of Archy's cause, for Negro and white antislavery newspapers in New England and New York covered the story with reports written by California Negro leaders. Many of these, such as Mifflin Wistar Gibbs, the Reverend Jeremiah B. Sanderson, and Peter Anderson, were experienced in the abolitionist movement and had worked with Frederick Douglass and William Lloyd Garrison before coming to California.

SIX

On the following day, Saturday, the charge against Stovall for kidnapping was dismissed in court on the technicality that the complaint had been issued over the signature of a deputy county clerk rather than a magistrate. This was not a serious setback to the campaign to free Archy. In fact, the kidnapping charge against Stovall had the quality of a maneuver rather than a major legal objective. Its purpose was to handicap Stovall in any legal manner possible while pursuing the major goal of freeing Archy. The plan was devised by a deputy clerk named David P. Belknap, not a prominent lawyer in 1858, but later a partner of Winans and Tompkins, who had been Archy's attorneys.

On Monday afternoon, March 8, the deadly serious phase of the struggle opened before County Judge T. W. Freelon. A fairly young man, Freelon undoubtedly felt the weight of his situation as not only lawyers but journalists speculated about the view he might take of the State Supreme Court decision. The San Francisco press carried editorial views in the papers issued between Archy's rescue-arrest on

Friday and the trial on Monday afternoon, and one newspaper advised Judge Freelon that "there is in the life of every man a time to 'make his mark'...and receive honorable mention in after times." This journal felt that the state constitution needed vindication from the "low estate into which it had fallen," while others blandly claimed that the Supreme Court decision could be ignored entirely. The consensus of press opinion clearly favored freedom for Archy. It must have been a difficult situation for a young man who, when not preoccupied with the duties of the bench, gave lectures on Thackeray and Dickens.

By one o'clock the courtroom and corridors of the city hall on Kearny Street were filled with interested persons, black and white, deeply engaged in discussion and argument. San Francisco was not without lawyers and proslavery residents who wanted Archy back in Stovall's possession. Archy, in the courtroom during the hearing, was described as neatly dressed and betraying no emotion at the proceedings. Stovall's attorneys were a Colonel James and again James H. Hardy, who had rushed from Sacramento to San Francisco to act as the prime lawyer for his client.

In Archy Lee's legal corner was a battery of talent that did credit to the efforts of the antislavery Negroes and whites of San Francisco. Attorneys Elisha O. Crosby, W. H. Tompkins, and Colonel E. D. Baker faced Judge Freelon on Archy's behalf. Crosby, a forty-niner, had been a member of the 1849 constitutional convention. He later became President Lincoln's

Minister to Guatemala. Tompkins, described as "one of the best lawyers in the state," became the first man to endow a chair at the University of California, which was the Agassiz professorship of Oriental literature and language.

Colonel Edward D. Baker was born of English Quaker parents who migrated to the United States and joined the moderately antislavery Campbellites. An old friend of Abraham Lincoln, he had also known his present opponent Hardy when both were young lawyers in central Illinois.

Colonel Baker was the oratorical giant of the trio defending Archy. He had become famous two years earlier for braving popular opinion and defending—when no one else would—the gambler Charles Cora in a murder case. He had said in his speech defending Cora that:

> There is no wretch so steeped in all the agonies of vice and crime, that I would not have a heart to listen to his cry, and a tongue to speak in his defense, though around his head all the wrath of public opinion should gather, and rage, and roar, and roll, as the ocean rolls around the rock. And if I ever forget, if I ever deny, that highest duty of my profession, may God palsy this arm and hush my voice forever.

At this time he was also a spokesman for the small and still unpopular Republican party in California, and his subsequent great contribution to keeping California in the Union and his death in battle during the Civil War are well recorded.

Forensic fireworks, however, had to wait. In his

haste to arrive in San Francisco, Hardy had left several documents in Sacramento. He also pleaded, with some justice, that he needed time to study new developments in the case. When he found himself facing Baker, the best orator of the California Bar, Hardy might have needed time for emotional adjustment as well. The case was continued to the following Monday, March 15.

On that date an expectant crowd was in Judge Freelon's court at one o'clock. There had been no slackening of interest in the Negro community. One newspaper reported that "Archy was in Court, and received the greetings of his friends and brethren with his accustomed composure." A dramatic performance was not to take place that day. For some reason, now unclear, a full-dress debate was not yet possible. Both sides agreed to a continuance to Wednesday, two days later.

Before this agreement was reached, however, Hardy made some remarks and a request that suggested his forthcoming legal strategy. He asked Judge Freelon to throw out the entire case on the grounds that the writ (granted by Freelon) by which Archy was taken from Stovall on the *Orizaba* was signed by James Riker, a Negro, and under California law (like that of most of the northern and all of the southern states) Negroes could not testify against white men in the courts.

The judge rejected Hardy's proposal, but his remark about Negro testimony warned Colonel Baker, who later was prepared to handle this legal point.

All participants in this historical drama were

present when Judge Freelon took his seat in the court that following Wednesday noon: Hardy and James on behalf of Stovall, and Baker and Tompkins to defend Archy. The courtroom again was packed with deeply interested persons of both races.

Preliminary exchanges between the attorneys led to an agreement that the validity of the writ of habeas corpus should be taken up first. Hardy opened the argument by repeating the claim that the writ should be dismissed. He supported his argument with several points: first, the law on Negro testimony made it invalid because Riker was a Negro; next, it might not have been proper for Freelon's court even to have presumed to have the power to issue such a writ (Judge Freelon interrupted Hardy to correct him); and finally Hardy showed great feeling when he made his last major point, that it was dangerous for a county court to ignore a State Supreme Court decision and behave as if it were still debatable in a lower court.

Hardy was interrupted several times by Archy's lawyers. At one point, when Hardy stated that writs could be misused to deprive a man of his slave property, Baker rejoined that a weakening of the power of the writ might also deprive a free man of his freedom. (There was a hint here that Archy's lawyers might be preparing to make the case that Archy was never a slave!)

Hardy concluded his presentation with the claim that a Supreme Court decision, even if it were wrong, must be accepted by lower courts. He digressed long enough to state publicly that he believed in Negro slavery and was "disgusted" by the "mobs" of free Negroes he saw on the wharves of San Francisco on the day Archy was rescued from the *Orizaba*. His final words were bitter about the way he and his case were treated by the "venal" press.

Colonel Baker next took the floor. He said he would not discuss the good or bad of slavery at the trial. He then claimed that the law excluding Negro testimony did not apply at the preliminary stage of the case. Colonel Baker must have known that by 1858 a few judges in the Bay Area for some time had been interpreting the law to allow Negro testimony.

Baker also claimed that what was called a Supreme Court decision in the Archy Lee case was not a Supreme Court decision at all. He maintained with incontestable logic that the Supreme Court was only an appeal court and that the case as it stood in Sacramento was not brought to the justices as an appeal; therefore, their action did not carry the authority of a higher court. Furthermore, Archy, in the strictly legal sense, was not a party to the case and could therefore ignore the decision.

Baker heaped scorn on the opinion of the Supreme Court justices. Their decision to suspend the constitution of the state of California because Stovall was a young man, in ill health and inexperienced, brought his strongest sarcasm. After all, asked Baker, how could the court be so unkind as to deny a weak young man the right to have his boots blacked and his morning coffee brought to his bed by his slave?

Baker concluded eloquently: he was prouder of being associated with the case than any he had ever worked on, and he hoped Judge Freelon would associate himself with this cause for freedom.

After Baker concluded, a series of exchanges took place between attorneys for both sides involving their respective wishes on procedure. Baker wanted to drop the matter of the merits of the writ and go on to general issues. Hardy opposed that at first but, surprisingly, changed his mind after a bit. The audience in the courtroom, expecting the discussion now to wheel around to the general issues of Archy's status, were in for a surprise. Once more Hardy asked Judge Freelon to dismiss the writ. He refused. After added exchanges, Baker turned to the judge and asked point blank for Archy's discharge. An astonished Judge Freelon then asked Hardy if he had any objection. The audience heard him say that he had none. Judge Freelon then freed Archy Lee.

SEVEN

What followed left the crowded courtroom stunned. Moments after Archy had been freed, as he was preparing to join his joyous compatriots, a United States marshal strode up and placed him under arrest. Archy, who had maintained his composure under weeks of immense strain, found this latest development too much to bear. As the marshal took hold of him, he shouted that he would never be taken back to slavery—he would die first. The iron self-discipline of Archy's friends also seemed about to crack. Angry voices filled the courtroom, but a rush to seize Archy, if contemplated, was impossible because the room was so tightly packed with people.

The marshal's action was based on the alleged legal grounds of the national fugitive slave law. Passed in 1850, this law was designed to effect the capture of Negroes fleeing across state lines from slave to free states. Colonel Baker examined the marshal's warrant for this new arrest and found it technically correct.

Baker now realized that Hardy had agreed to Archy's release only because he had already planned this new approach. In fact, he had arranged for this second arrest that morning. Perhaps because he sensed he was going to lose in the courts of San Francisco, he was now making the Archy Lee case a federal one.

The bedlam in the courtroom poured out into Kearny Street in front of the courthouse. Colonel Baker, now readjusting his strategy, went up to Archy to reassure him. Urging Archy to go along with the marshal and his assisting officers, he told him that he would not be harmed. Press reports suggest that Archy felt only partly reassured by Baker's words. If the Negro leadership had rushed the police on the streets of San Francisco that afternoon, Archy undoubtedly would have cooperated. But this did not happen. Negro organizers of the campaign to free Archy still had hopes in Baker and the law. Nevertheless, rank-and-file Negroes in the streets behaved as if their confidence in the law had been shaken.

Archy had to be taken from the city hall on Kearny Street to the Merchants Exchange Building on Oregon Street, where Commissioner Johnston had his office. The excited throng that surrounded and trailed Archy and the police numbered at times five to six hundred persons. The din was deafening. Many of those following Archy shouted at police and argued with each other. Some proslavery whites, perhaps by plan, formed a cordon around Archy and the officers to help push the balky Negro down the streets to the commissioner's office. Around this ring large numbers of enraged blacks were also pushing and shouting. The marshal and his posse went from

Kearny to Washington Street, down Washington to Montgomery, from Montgomery to Jackson, down Jackson to Battery, and along Battery to Oregon. They had to push and strong-arm their way through the crowd. Along the way some Negroes shouted that Archy should be freed on the street. Whites quarreled with whites, and some Negroes got into angry arguments with whites. Several of the black men along the way begged the police to let Archy go.

Remarkably, this explosive situation terminated with only two arrests—both of angry Negroes. One of them was a preacher who had come from Marysville to attend the trial, which suggests how deeply and widely this issue was felt among Negroes throughout the state. The closest the melee came to a race riot was when a particularly incensed black man was attacked by a white one and struck back. The sight of a Negro hitting a white offended the notions of racial etiquette held by some whites, and they attacked him en masse. The police managed to rescue him.

While Archy was surrounded by the marshal and his posse, the crowd was so dense that he was buffeted about considerably. He was described as having bruises when he arrived at the commissioner's office but, as one paper put it, "Archy, to his credit be it said, dealt manfully about him when pushed and crowded." The proslavery *San Francisco Herald* called Archy's behavior "mulish."

EIGHT

United States Commissioner George Pen Johnston must have been puzzled and disturbed the Wednesday morning Stovall and his lawyers brought him an affidavit compelling him to arrest Archy as a fugitive slave. He knew—as did all of San Francisco—that that same afternoon Stovall was going through the serious motions of a court trial before Judge Freelon in order to keep Archy. (At a later date in legal history this would be considered capricious behavior at the expense of public funds. But gold rush California was not known for its legal niceties.)

Johnston may have been pained at this questionable procedure and more than pained to discover his decision nine weeks earlier had failed to disengage him from this awkward case. At that time he had concluded that Archy was not a fugitive from Mississippi. As a southerner and a Democrat, Johnston was associated politically and personally with the strong proslavery wing of the Democratic party. Undoubtedly Stovall's supporters knew this and hoped for special treatment at his hands. But Johnston was also gentler by nature than most of the aggressive, fire-eating, proslavery southerners. For example, some years earlier he had tried to curb dueling in California. Within the limits of his cultural environment he was a fair man.

Archy finally reached Commissioner Johnston, who decided to have a hearing the next day at two o'clock. Bruised but unbowed, Archy Lee went back to the county jail.

Forty-five minutes before the appointed time of the hearing, the commissioner's chamber was full of spectators. Colonel Baker asked for a delay to obtain evidence and to attend to another case he had later that day. Over Hardy's objections, Johnston granted a one-day continuance as a matter of courtesy.

Even prior to the first session before the United States commissioner, Archy's lawyers had decided on a parallel strategy. While Archy was being escorted that tumultuous Wednesday from Freelon's court to the commissioner's office, his attorneys Crosby and Tompkins filed a suit against Stovall for $2,500 damages for assault, battery, and false imprisonment.

Friday afternoon Commissioner Johnston had arranged to preside over the hearing in the courtroom of Judge Hall McAllister. Because of some novel feature of the seating arrangements, Archy, although he had become something of an amateur expert on the layout of courtrooms, came in and sat down in Judge McAllister's accustomed seat. The roomful of spectators exploded in laughter. When it subsided and Archy had taken his appropriate place in the courtroom, the debate began.

It soon became evident that Hardy was building his case entirely on the national fugitive slave law and was claiming that Archy was a fugitive, not from Stovall's control in Sacramento, but from Mississippi. This law denied a runaway Negro any right to counsel, and on this basis Stovall insisted that Baker's presence was illegal. Hardy said, "Archy is property and nothing more, and he has no more right to be heard in this proceeding than has a bale of goods or a horse."

Colonel Baker did not quarrel with Hardy's explanation of the federal law but stated he still had a role to play in the proceedings because it remained to be proved that Archy was, in truth, a bona fide fugitive slave. He noted that in a famous case in Boston, the Negro Anthony Burns had had the privilege of counsel. Commissioner Johnston ruled that Archy also had that right. As proceedings continued, frequent outbursts of applause by pro-Stovall elements in the audience had to be silenced by the marshal.

His right to speak established, Baker proceeded to make his most effective points. He produced records of the Sacramento hearings in which Stovall had *never* mentioned Archy as a fugitive from Mississippi and in which Johnston had removed himself from the case because the national fugitive slave law was not involved. Baker next produced an affidavit from Archy claiming that he was never a slave in Mississippi. A second affidavit, from a John P. Zane, was presented to prove that Zane had known Stovall in Sacramento and was under the impression that Archy had never been a slave. It also claimed that Stovall had intended to become a permanent resident in California.

Commissioner Johnston now had two contradictory sets of data confronting him. Baker's request for a continuance probably came as much-needed relief from his judicial agony. The commissioner granted a continuance to March 29, ten days later. This was the longest one that had yet been granted in the history of the case.

The fact that Stovall's position was being compromised beyond repair by the self-contradictory documents produced by Baker did not bring much comfort to George Pen Johnston. That same month his wing of the Democratic party was trying to push a vicious anti-Negro-immigration bill through the state assembly. His pending decision could keep a Negro in California when his compatriots were attempting to drive Negroes out of the state.

NINE

The ten days between hearings were not uneventful: Charles A. Stovall left town. He accomplished his departure with so much secrecy that the press, caught off guard, was chagrined at having missed a good story. Stovall was believed to have sailed on the *Sonora*, which departed from San Francisco on Monday morning, March 22. (Perhaps he boarded her from a rowboat in the middle of the bay.)

The circumstances of Stovall's departure spawned some improbable rumors. One said Stovall had sold Archy before he left. (Everyone knew, of course, that only a feebleminded person would have considered such a transaction.) Another had it that Archy was on a revenue cutter headed for Panama. The soundest was that someone had realistically warned Stovall he was in great danger of being charged with perjury. There were those who would have been delighted with just such a prospect.

During this pause, several newspapers amused their readers at Hardy's expense and his anger was unbounded. He accused them of being corrupt and of taking monies from any side of an issue. One newspaper retorted that it was in rather bad taste for a member of the legal profession in California to raise this issue, since attorneys were vulnerable on this score.

Stovall's departure did not lessen the work of the Negro community. However, the full story of its efforts may never be known. The executive committee of the Colored Convention had published a newspaper called the *Mirror of the Times* in the 1850s, but research has not revealed any numbers for the period of the Archy Lee case. Yet it is possible occasionally to get a glimpse of the committee's work. For example, the March 26 issue of the *California Chronicle* noted in the corner of one page that $97 had been raised in Nevada City for Archy's cause. The story also persists that the famous Mammy Pleasant gave aid to Archy.

While raising funds was of vital importance to the executive committee of the Colored Convention, its public image was of equal importance. The numerous trials, to which a great number of Negroes came religiously, created situations pregnant with disorder. While serious trouble never occurred—and the nearest thing to it took place after Judge Freelon freed Archy and the marshal rearrested him—the sight of so many freedom-seeking Negroes upset many San Franciscans. Uncle Tom never looked like this. Absence of docility equaled disorder. Even the *Alta California*, which seemed to take a middle-of-the-road position, in an effort to be dramatically descriptive in its reports gave an impression of heaving turbulence.

As a result, the troubled executive committee of the Colored Convention drew up a statement to describe its true posture. Published by the *Daily Evening Bulletin*, whose record of sympathy to the Negro was long known, the statement read:

> EDITOR EVENING BULLETIN:—We respectfully ask permission to publish in your columns the following Card to the Public, which has been caused by the times:
>
> At a public meeting of the colored citizens of San Francisco, held in Zion Church, on 25th March, the undersigned were appointed a committee to publish a card setting forth the views of the colored people of this city, and their true position, in relation to the slavery under which we live.
>
> There has been a disposition manifested by a portion of the press in this city, to misrepresent us, by characterizing us as a rebellious and turbulent class of persons, who disregard the laws of our country, when we come in contact with them, or when they happen to oppose our peculiar views. Now we wish to inform our friends and the public generally, that we are a law-loving and law-abiding class of persons, who have always quietly submitted to the unjust enactments that have been imposed upon us, in this our common country, from time to time. We have been the subjects of innumerable wrongs without any just cause, yet we have borne up under them with scarcely a murmur, and can appeal with pride to our character and standing throughout this entire State, and point to our industry, integrity and moral worth.
>
> It has been publicly asserted that we had counseled and determined to rescue the boy Archy from the custody of the officers who had him in charge and that we had no confidence in the legal tribunals of this State—or in the United States Commissioner, before whom he is to be tried.
>
> All of this, we pronounce an unqualified falsehood, gotten up by our enemies for the purpose of making

political capital against us in the community. As a class, we are a liberty-loving people, who are deeply interested in whatever pertains to the welfare of mankind. In the case of Archy, we feel that we are maintaining the laws of the State of California, and ask for his liberation upon just and legal grounds, believing that he is rightly entitled to his freedom, which we are interested in securing according to law, and which we will leave no proper means untried to accomplish. We are well satisfied that the reflecting portion of the people are disposed to act justly by us in this case, and award us all that we merit—that of being a quiet and orderly class of people.

TEN

On the long-awaited March 29, the case resumed before Commissioner Johnston. At one o'clock the proceedings had barely begun when they almost ended. A large chunk of plaster came loose from the wall and fell in the midst of the attorneys. Fortunately, no one was hurt. When the nervous audience settled down, the debate began. This time Hardy asked for a continuance. He based his request on a curious affidavit from William D. Stovall, the brother of Charles. In the first paragraph its credibility became questionable, for there this newly-heard-from Stovall stated that he was "not interested either directly or indirectly in the matter named above" (the Archy Lee case). He went on to tell the story of Archy's assault on a white man in Mississippi and his subsequent flight from the state. He claimed that Archy was a slave. He described his brother's ill health and the decision to go to California. From William Stovall's affidavit, it appeared that he went with Charles. This was the first notice of another Stovall on the scene. The big surprise was the statement that Charles, evidently accidentally, ran into Archy at the crossing of the North Platte some eight hundred miles from Mississippi. With whom Archy was traveling and what he was doing is never stated in this affidavit, nor in any earlier statements by the frailer Stovall. It is allegedly at this point that the Stovall brothers overtook Archy and carried him on to California.

William Stovall's affidavit stated that Charles Stovall had left San Francisco to go to Mississippi for documents to prove that Archy was a slave. At the conclusion of the reading, Hardy confirmed the reason for Charles Stovall's departure and asked for a continuance until these documents arrived. Commissioner Johnston refused Hardy's request, saying he would explain later. The case was continued for that day.

The courtroom then heard more affidavits and even some testimony by witnesses who were there in person to give it. Two pro-Stovall supporters from Sacramento presented an affidavit in which they claimed to have known Stovall in Mississippi and to be certain that Archy was a slave there. They also supported the story of Archy as a runaway from Mississippi who was "captured" at the crossing of the North Platte.

Next came a droll bit of testimony from the police officer who had charge of Archy in the Sacramento jail. A witness for Stovall, he said that Archy himself had declared he belonged to Stovall. Archy was also said to have commented on his attack on a white man in Mississippi, leading to the officer having asked him if Negroes were not killed in Mississippi for attacking white men. Archy is supposed to have replied, "Why, Lord bless your soul, master, I didn't give 'em a chance."

The dense crowd in the courtroom was rewarded with more performers than were paraded in any previous hearing. A series of witnesses for Archy took the stand. They were all from Sacramento and had had contact with Archy, as well as Stovall, either in Sacramento or on the plains crossing in 1857. The substance of their testimony contributed to Baker's claim that Archy was not a runaway and that Stovall's posture as a traveler was fictitious. One of the witnesses testified that he had hired Archy to do odd jobs in Sacramento, another stated that he had gone to Stovall's school, and a third witness introduced a third character by declaring that still another Stovall brother had been on the trip to California. Perhaps most significant of all was one of the last bits of evidence introduced by Archy's defense. It was simply Charles Stovall's advertisement in the *Sacramento Age* announcing his private school and giving the opening date and tuition. Stovall asked five dollars per month "in advance." Such an institution and such long-term fees strongly suggest that Stovall was not a mere traveler through California.

The case was adjourned to the next day, Tuesday, at one o'clock. The following afternoon the courtroom was crowded as usual. Brother William Stovall, on the stand, was interrogated by attorney Tompkins. Their exchange revealed a strong possibility that the Stovalls were concealing a family quarrel of some kind in which Archy had a role. As Tompkins pressed this line of investigation, William Stovall was hesitant; at one point he stated that he did not believe private family matters were of any concern to the court. But it did come out that he would *not* say with certainty that Archy was a runaway. In fact, from the testimony of all Stovall witnesses, the feeling emerged that Archy's relations with the Stovall brothers were friendly during the meandering journey west—atypical of American fugitive-captor relationships. (From other evidence this writer suspects that there had been a fight over slave ownership among the Stovalls before they left Mississippi.)

In the course of the Stovall interrogation the courtroom almost erupted into violence. Tompkins had been trying to draw out Stovall about possible family quarrels. Hardy objected. After one exchange Tompkins mistakenly assumed that Hardy had withdrawn his objections. Tompkins said as much to Stovall. Hardy jumped up calling Tompkins a liar and rushed at him. Tompkins rose in his seat. Men hurried in and held Hardy back, and Commissioner Johnston had to enter the melee to settle matters. He was furious. But he did quiet things, and apologies were made to the court by both attorneys. The electrified audience anticipated bloodshed because it appeared that Hardy carried a poorly concealed gun.

The story of Hardy's gun lingered on. For about a week after the flare-up the press printed references to Hardy's alleged possession of a gun in the courtroom and noted his denials. Certainly, carrying concealed weapons into the courtrooms and legislative assemblies of the early West was not unknown.

This session concluded with Hardy's asking for a continuance for *sixty* days because several of his witnesses were absent. It was denied, but a continuance was granted for Tuesday, a week later.

After this momentarily explosive session, an *Alta California* reporter wrote the first relatively long interview with Archy to appear in any paper. Full of interest and the ring of truth, it reads:

> ARCHY'S STORY—We yesterday [Tuesday, March 30, 1858] saw Archy for a few moments and questioned him about the manner in which he left Mississippi. He said he was born in Pike county, Mississippi, and is about nineteen years old. January last he was in the possession of Charles Stovall, but there was a dispute in the family about the negroes, and about him among others. Charles Stovall lived in Carroll county; he (Archy) was working in the adjoining county of Choctaw, at a mill belonging to Mr. Stovall. One night a colored man came to him and requested him to go to the bridge which separates the two counties, to see Mr. Smiley. After much objection he went. Mr. Smiley was on the Choctaw side, and tried to persuade Archy to go to some distant place with him. Archy refused. Smiley then told him to say nothing of what had passed and said he would give him $5; but after looking in his pocketbook, said he had no money and invited Archy across the bridge, where he would get some money and give him $5. Archy went across, and was soon seized by Smiley and Carroll Stovall (the latter a cousin of Charles), who started to take him off. Smiley told him that the sheriff of Carroll county was there and had an attachment for him. Archy told Smiley he was not the Sheriff, and then breaking away, he drew a knife and stabbed Smiley twice in [the] left breast, inflicting two

wounds—not of a serious character. He then ran back across the bridge and was not troubled by Smiley. He was afterwards told that the Sheriff of Carroll county was there, but refused to act; and he was also told that Smiley got well and that no legal proceedings were ever taken on account of the stabbing. The next morning Mr. Aaron Hart, who had charge of the sawmill, told him to go away from the house and hide in the bushes. He did so, and a negro took out his dinner to him. In the evening, a negro came and told him that he must go away from there, and Archy went off with him to Middletown. Near that place, Charles A. Stovall appeared with a buggy and took him and drove away with him and took him to the plantation of John Carnes in Cape Girardeau County, Mo. and left him there. They crossed the Mississippi river at Memphis in a ferry boat. Charles Stovall left him with Carnes and went away; and several months later Wm. Stovall came and got him. Archy says that Mr. Simon Stovall and Mr. Hart, in Mississippi, and Mr. Carnes and Mr. Hunter in Missouri, know the truth of what he says about Charles Stovall taking him from Mississippi to Missouri.

ELEVEN

Commissioner Johnston opened the next scene of the drama on Tuesday, April 6, exactly three months after Archy's first arrest in Hackett House, Sacramento. Archy had spent most of this time in jails, a fact not overlooked by Johnston, as his opening remarks in the United States circuit courtroom suggest. A week earlier the commissioner had denied Hardy's request for a sixty-day continuance. He now explained why, and the statement was a sharp criticism of Stovall and his lawyers as well as a hint of his forthcoming decision. To a packed courtroom he spoke of the length of time it was taking for the case to drag through the courts. He reminded Stovall's lawyers that weeks before, when he had faced the case for the second time, he had told them to take a continuance to investigate the case fully and at that time *they* were against any continuances. He felt that Charles Stovall's sudden departure cast a shadow on his claims and that since, under the national fugitive slave law, bail was not allowed, Archy would be confined far beyond "the letter or the spirit" of that law if a continuance were granted. With this denial Johnston revealed his mounting impatience, and the proceedings began.

A man named E. H. Baker took the stand as a witness for Stovall, but although he had known the Stovalls in Mississippi and Archy as a slave, his evidence proved more harmful than helpful to the Stovall case. His testimony strengthened the impression that Archy was far from a fugitive. Rather, it gave force to the belief that Archy was in Missouri by Stovall collusion and that William Stovall had taken Archy to Kansas and then gone to the North Platte, where he joined his brother Charles. Baker actually declared that he had not heard any suggestion that Archy was a fugitive when he was still in Mississippi nor while he was traveling with Charles to meet William at the crossing of the North Platte.

If Archy were truly a fugitive, in 1857 the Kansas territory would have been the last place in the world to take him. It was full of militant antislavery men who would have helped Archy to escape without hesitation. Indeed, Archy's decision to try for freedom in California might have been formed during his sojourn in Kansas.

Although the Stovall defense was disintegrating, Hardy then made a speech—essentially a review of all his witnesses' testimony—to prove Archy was a runaway. Tompkins followed him with a review of all previous hearings where Charles Stovall failed even to hint that Archy was a fugitive. Colonel Baker came next, saying much the same. The case was continued to the next day.

At noon Wednesday, April 7, proceedings opened

without Hardy, who had gone to Sacramento, presumably to obtain more evidence. In his place G. J. Whelan represented Stovall but contributed little to the direction of the case. This was Colonel E. D. Baker's day. He began by discussing the differences between the American fugitive slave laws of 1793 and 1850. He hinted broadly and eloquently that the principles of freedom were not strengthened in the process of the change. While Baker was telling Commissioner Johnston of the immense power and responsibility Johnston had been given by the 1850 law, the annoyed Whelan interrupted. He stated that he did not believe that the commissioner had any trial responsibilities. All he needed to do, according to Whelan, was place the Negro in bondage if a white man claimed him as his fugitive property. This remark provoked Johnston to make his own interruption. He said:

> It seems a monstrous doctrine that on one affidavit I should send a man off to be taken to another state as a slave, ostensibly to be tried by another tribunal, but really under such circumstances that he would have no remedy if taken to another state and put under the hammer at a moment's notice.

This comment sat badly with the fire-eating southerners in the audience. For them Johnston would forever be a traitor to the South.

But Colonel Baker had more to say. He made a brilliant review of the law as it bore on the case and a scathing commentary on Hardy's interpretation of the law. He derided the image of Stovall as a frail traveler and of Archy as a fugitive. He played havoc with the story of Stovall as a Johnny-come-lately fugitive slave chaser.

Stovall's belated decision to shift to the fugitive charge was probably fatal to his case. Baker also dwelt on an issue called *comity* that was raised from time to time by the Stovall defense. Under comity, states and nations are expected to respect each other's laws; and therefore Hardy expected Mississippi slave law to be honored in favor of Stovall. Colonel Baker agreed that comity deserved respect but *never* at the expense of the constitution. He further argued against comity, first with oratory by declaring that never should it be respected more than human liberty, then with satire by pointing out that there was never any evidence submitted in any of the hearings that Mississippi was a slave state. He concluded his performance, and performance it was, by hammering at the weakest point in Hardy's argument—the image of Archy as a fugitive slave. He roused a sense of nationalism in the hearts of his hearers as he dwelt on the methods of the Stovall defense. His closing words were, "And so they have made sport, game, of the dearest and highest principles of our government."

One reporter stated that he found words inadequate to portray the great eloquence of Baker's address. Another noted that many eyes were moist with tears when Baker concluded. There was subdued applause when he sat down. Whelan rose to say that he was not feeling well and would not take the floor. Commissioner Johnston then requested that the attorneys present him with their final briefs by the end of that week. He said he would render a decision the following Tuesday, April 13.

By the end of the week the press had copies of the briefs, which were different both in argument and style. Tompkins wrote the brief for Archy; it was a straightforward legal statement. The main point was that Archy did not bear any of the characteristics of a fugitive, and the manner in which he came to California proved it. Hardy's brief was more flamboyant. One newspaper described it as "in the stump speech style." He called Archy's witnesses "beyond belief," declared that too many people at the time were under the influence of Mrs. Stowe's book *Uncle Tom's Cabin*, and dwelt heavily on the rights of private property.

The day for the commissioner's decision came closer. The outcome was still in doubt, but further legal maneuver by either side seemed ended. Much of the press thought that the commissioner would free Archy out of simple respect for logic. Earlier in the case one pro-Archy paper had hinted that a decision for freedom might make a congressman out of Johnston because of Republican support. Few envied the commissioner, whose opinions seemed to lean toward Colonel Baker, but whose personal sentiments were in the Hardy camp.

Johnston, who was to deliver his opinion on April 13,

decided to delay it until the next day and make it a public event with press, public, and attorneys for both sides hearing it together.

In a sense, a symbolic moment was lost when the commissioner decided on the delay, for on Tuesday the *Orizaba* sailed back into San Francisco harbor on its return from Panama.

TWELVE

At two o'clock on Wednesday, April 14, a large crowd gathered in the United States circuit courtroom to hear the commissioner's decision. The commissioner made a long statement. He said he felt that the State Supreme Court had never decided the question of Archy Lee and in reality did not have the power to do so; that in a fugitive slave case legal defense for the fugitive could be allowed; that he, the commissioner, could deal officially with the case only if it were a genuine fugitive slave case; that all events involving Archy and all relations among Archy and the Stovalls between Mississippi and the California border did not support the contention that Archy was a fugitive; that running away *within* the boundaries of California did not make Archy a fugitive even under the national fugitive slave act; and that, therefore, Archy was not a fugitive but a free man.

At the conclusion of his statement, Commissioner George Pen Johnston was warmly applauded by Archy's jubilant friends, but a moment later they suffered one last scare. Archy was not present at this hearing, and few knew that the commissioner had asked that he be freed from the jailhouse rather than from the hearing room. When the audience suddenly realized that Archy was not there, some suspected foul play, and a murmur arose. The mystery was rapidly cleared up when Colonel Baker went out into the hall and told James Riker, the man whose name was on several of the affidavits, and Peter Anderson, one of the most important leaders of the Colored Convention movement, that United States Marshal Soloman had a voucher to free Archy.

A joyous group led by Colonel Baker, Riker, and Anderson walked to the jailhouse on Kearny Street to receive Archy. The good word spread quickly on the streets between the United States circuit court and the jail, for hundreds were there to welcome Archy. The keeper was reported to have gone to his cell and unlocked it saying, "Archy, my boy, you're all right; you're a free man now; pick up your duds and be off; your friends are waiting for you outside."

When Archy appeared on the street he was pulled and hauled and congratulated. Everyone was trying to shake his hand. Colonel Baker was described as looking at the proceedings with a pleased expression. One man tried to get everybody to yell "three cheers" but was shushed by the other Negroes, who were determined to achieve a quiet decorum.

Soon a carriage drove up and Archy and a group of his friends got in and rode off swiftly towards the sandhills to the west. One reporter wondered why Archy was hurried off this way and came to the sensible conclusion that the Negroes felt that "white man berry unsartin." Looking to his right down Vallejo Street, Archy could have seen the *Orizaba* riding anchor in San Francisco Bay.

EPILOGUE

When Archy Lee rode away from the Kearny Street courtroom where he had just gained his freedom, he had little idea of his destination. According to one source, he went directly to the home of Mammy Pleasant to hide until he could be sure that California justice would not change its mind again. If this is true, Mrs. Pleasant was not at home to greet Archy; her biographer claims she had left California a few weeks earlier to assist John Brown in his Harpers Ferry plans. Furthermore, Archy did not really seem to hide because a few days later he was reported as being "rapturously cheered" while attending a victory celebration in his honor given by the San Francisco Negro community at the African Methodist Episcopal Zion Church on Pacific Street.

Another purpose of this gathering was to make plans for a general migration of black people to Victoria, British Columbia. Economic opportunities had expanded there following the Fraser River gold rush, and a friendly reception was assured by local government officials. When Archy's friends offered to pay his expenses for the move to Victoria, he probably decided without hesitation to join the migration. For the Negro community it was important that Archy, their one symbol of victory in an otherwise depressing year, leave the uncertain freedom of California and try for a new life in Canada.

Little is known of Archy Lee's later life. He returned from British Columbia after the Civil War started, as did many expatriate Negroes, in the hope of finding a better life in their native land. In December 1862 the *Pacific Appeal*, a weekly San Francisco Negro newspaper, reported that Archy was working as a barber in Washoe, Nevada.

The next word about Archy comes eleven years later, in November 1873, and it strikes a sad note. He is reported by the San Francisco Negro press, as well as the Sacramento white newspapers, to have been found lying seriously ill on a bank of the American River. He had buried himself in the sand, probably in a fever, and was refusing any help. He wished to be left alone and "not bodder anybody," as the press reported it. Archy Lee was then in his early thirties, and one can only guess at what personal and psychological defeats he may have suffered by 1873. However, he was persuaded to allow himself to be taken to the county hospital. Although the only further news of Archy was that he had died there, the usually reliable *Sacramento Daily Union* failed to list his death in its end-of-the-year vital statistics.

A question may arise in the reader's mind concerning the real nature of the relationship between Archy Lee

BISHOP JOHN J. MOORE, D.D.

John J. Moore

A national leader in the A.M.E. Zion Church, John J. Moore took up Archy Lee's cause and volunteered his church in San Francisco as a meeting place for Archy Lee's supporters. (Image courtesy of the New York City Public Library, from Hood, J. W. *One Hundred Years of the African Methodist*, Sc Rare 287-H)

Mary Ellen "Mammy" Pleasant at 87 years of age, ca. 1905

Mary Ellen "Mammy" Pleasant, perhaps the best-known African American civil rights campaigner and entrepreneur in late-nineteenth-century San Francisco, is said to have provided aid and refuge for Archy Lee. (Image courtesy of the Bancroft Library, University of California, Berkeley, BANC PIC: 1905.0002-POR)

Mifflin Westal [Wistar] Gibbs, ca. 1873

A businessman and civil rights activist, Gibbs passionately argued for Archy Lee's freedom. Gibbs would later move to Arkansas, where he became a judge and a leader in the state Republican Party. (Image courtesy of the British Columbia Archives, Photo #B-01601)

from *The Negro in California History* mural series by Hale Woodruff and Charles Alston, 1949

The Negro in California History was created by African American artists Hale Woodruff and Charles Alston for the lobby of the Golden State Mutual Insurance Company, a black-owned business serving mostly African Americans in Los Angeles. This panel, the second of two, was created by Woodruff to depict the period from 1850 to 1949. In addition to portraying black laborers constructing the Golden Gate Bridge, mining for gold, and riding for the Pony Express, the mural depicts organizations and activists from the vigorous civil rights movement of nineteenth-century California. The progressive newspaper *The Elevator* (left), the Convention of the Colored Citizens of the State of California (just right of center), and Mary Ellen "Mammy" Pleasant (slightly left of center, wearing a white head-covering), among others, also figure in the work. (Image courtesy of Golden State Mutual Life Insurance and the African American Museum and Library at Oakland, Civil Rights collection pho. 94.850.CV-021B)

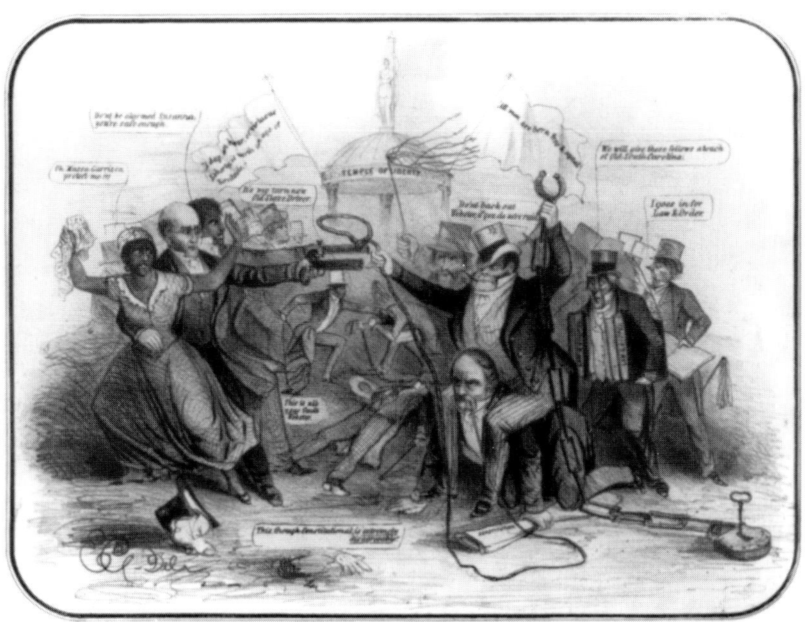

PRACTICAL ILLUSTRATION OF THE FUGITIVE SLAVE LAW.

"Practical Illustration of the Fugitive Slave Law," 1851

As residents of a free state, Californians could not own slaves, so a crucial aspect of Archy Lee's case was determining whether he was a runaway slave and thus the rightful property of Charles Stovall under the Fugitive Slave Act of 1793. This cartoon illustrates the intensity of the national political debate surrounding the passage and enforcement of the later 1850 Fugitive Slave Law. A compromise between northern and southern states to strengthen the rarely enforced 1793 act, it forbade the aiding or sheltering of escaped slaves anywhere in the nation. In the illustration, Attorney General Daniel Webster, who pledged to vigorously impose the law, is being ridden by a slave catcher. To the left is the abolitionist William Lloyd Garrison, who is protectively embracing a runaway slave. Banners declaring "A day, an hour, of virtuous Liberty is worth an age of Servitude" and "All men are born free and equal" flutter overhead. (Image courtesy of the Library of Congress, PC/US-1851.C619, no. 42)

"Effects of the Fugitive-Slave-Law" by Theodore Kauffman, 1850

This lithograph, a dramatic depiction of a posse of white men firing upon four unarmed black men, is a clear condemnation of the 1850 Fugitive Slave Law. The black men could either be escaped slaves or freedman mistaken for slaves, perhaps assisting in an escape (the attire of the center figure hints at this). The white men, most probably hoping to profit from the fee awarded to slave catchers after the Fugitive Slave Act was passed, are ready in their excitement to shoot any black-skinned person. Quotes from the Bible and the Declaration of Independence flank the title of the image and reinforce the artist's message. (Image courtesy of the Library of Congress, PC/US-1850.H698, no. 1)

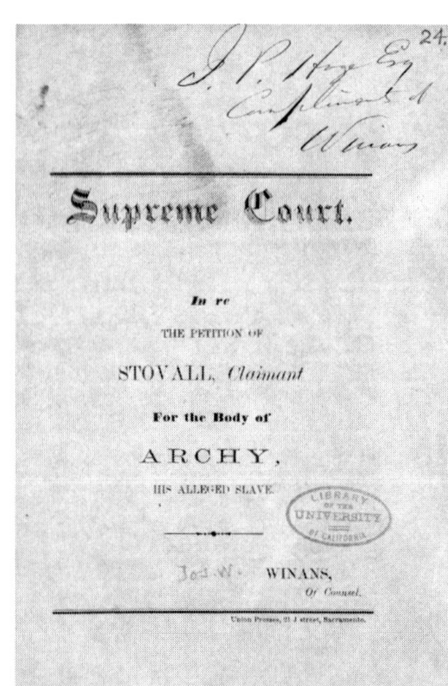

Supreme Court.

In re

THE PETITION OF

STOVALL, *Claimant*

For the Body of

ARCHY,

HIS ALLEGED SLAVE.

WINANS,

Of Counsel.

Union Presses, 21 J street, Sacramento.

"In re the Petition of Stovall, Claimant for the Body of Archy, His Alleged Slave," 1858

This is the title page to a pamphlet containing an argument before California's Supreme Court presented by Joseph W. Winans, one of Archy Lee's many lawyers. Winans argued that allowing Stovall to keep Archy Lee as a slave would set a precedent, allowing slavery to take hold in California. This, he said, would devalue "free labor" and, in particular, harm the state's miners. (Image courtesy of the Bancroft Library, University of California, Berkeley, BANC xF858.C21 v. 18:24)

"ARCHY."

TO THE FRIENDS

......OF THE......

CONSTITUTION AND LAWS.

THE COMMITTEE APPOINTED BY THE Colored People having expended a large amount, and incurred heavy obligations in prosecuting and defending the case in the Courts of Sacramento, Stockton and San Francisco, and believing the principles to be vindicated are those which should interest all lovers of right and justice, independent of complexion, respectfully solicit contributions for this object, which will be faithfully appropriated, if left with

m20-3t E. J. JOHNSON, 184 Clay street.

"Archy" advertisement directed to "the friends of the Constitution and Laws," 1858

Archy Lee's case galvanized many of San Francisco's African Americans and abolitionists. They helped to cover his legal expenses, were a constant presence at his trials, and organized dockside patrols to ensure Charles Stovall didn't kidnap and transport Archy Lee out of California by way of San Francisco's Golden Gate. This advertisement from the *California Daily Chronicle* solicits the help of "all lovers of right and justice, independent of complexion." (Image courtesy of California State University, Sacramento, Digital Archives, Image #01057)

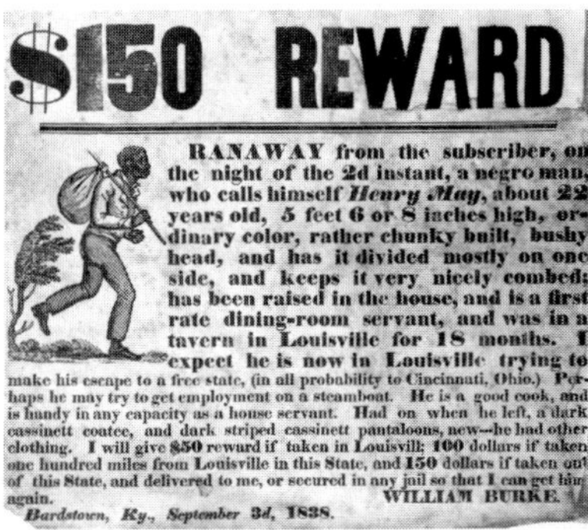

$150 REWARD

RANAWAY from the subscriber, on the night of the 2d instant, a negro man, who calls himself *Henry May*, about 22 years old, 5 feet 6 or 8 inches high, ordinary color, rather chunky built, bushy head, and has it divided mostly on one side, and keeps it very nicely combed; has been raised in the house, and is a first rate dining-room servant, and was in a tavern in Louisville for 18 months. I expect he is now in Louisville trying to make his escape to a free state, (in all probability to Cincinnati, Ohio.) Perhaps he may try to get employment on a steamboat. He is a good cook, and is handy in any capacity as a house servant. Had on when he left, a dark cassinett coatee, and dark striped cassinett pantaloons, new--he had other clothing. I will give $50 reward if taken in Louisvill; 100 dollars if taken one hundred miles from Louisville in this State, and 150 dollars if taken out of this State, and delivered to me, or secured in any jail so that I can get him again.

WILLIAM BURKE.

Bardstown, Ky., September 3d, 1838.

Runaway slave poster, 1838

Bulletins and posters offering large sums of money for the capture of escaped slaves enticed "slave catchers" and law enforcement. This example from 1838 offers from $50 to $150 for the "taking" of Henry May, described as a "a first rate dining-room servant." The iconic image of a runaway slave with a bindle over one shoulder was frequently used in these posters. The artist Mallette Dean brilliantly appropriated it for the cover of the 1969 edition of Archy Lee and it also appears as the cover of this edition. (Image courtesy of the Library of Congress, Printed Ephemera Collection; Portfolio 22, Folder 12b)

Merchants' Exchange, Battery and Washington, San Francisco, by George R. Fardon, ca. 1854

The Merchants' Exchange Building in San Francisco served as a U.S. District Court during Archy Lee's time in the city and was where he was finally disentangled from Charles Stovall and from the state and federal legal system. (Image courtesy of the Bancroft Library, University of California, Berkeley, BANC 1905.17500 v.3:26-ACB)

Private School
FOR BOYS AND GIRLS
BY
C. A. STOVALL,
K street, near 7th. To commence on Monday, the 12th of October, 1857.
Terms—$5 per month, in advance. o9

Advertisement for C. A. Stovall's private school for boys and girls, 1857

Not long after arriving in California, Charles Stovall repeatedly placed this advertisement for a private school in the *Sacramento Age* newspaper. In the trial it was used as evidence that, contrary to his claim, his status in California was not that of a traveler and he was therefore not entitled to hold a slave in the state. (Image courtesy of the U.S. National Archives and Records Administration, ARC #295963)

Untitled [nineteenth-century San Francisco], ca. 1860s

This cartoon plays on nineteenth-century San Francisco's reputation as a frenzied, ethnically diverse port. A poster to the right advertises the Jenny Lind Theater, which in 1855 was converted to San Francisco's City Hall. The building housed the sheriff's department, where Archy Lee was brought upon his arrival in San Francisco, accompanied by a large audience of the "colored population of the town...thronging the City Hall in large numbers." (Image courtesy of the California Historical Society, FN-19321)

Peter H. Burnett, California's first governor

Peter H. Burnett acted as governor of California before serving two years on the California Supreme Court. A southerner, Burnett wrote the opinion sending Archy Lee temporarily back into slavery. (Image courtesy of the Bancroft Library, University of California, Berkeley, BANC PIC: 1905.0002)

Colonel E. D. Baker, 1861

Edward Dickinson Baker acted as Archy Lee's legal counsel. He would later serve in the U.S. Senate and die as a Union colonel in the Civil War. (Image courtesy of the Bancroft Library, University of California, Berkeley, BANC PIC: 1963.002:0494-B) and Charles Stovall. For an answer to this, one must make surmises based on knowledge of the antebellum South and slavery in the United States. The available record suggests that on the surface the personal relationship between Stovall and Lee was not hostile. It often happened in the antebellum South that a planter's son grew up with a slave boy as a friend and companion in his early years, and this was probably the situation of Archy and Stovall, who were not far apart in age. All the testimony about the journey from Cape Girardeau, Missouri, to Sacramento lacks any suggestion of threat or violence between the Stovalls and Archy Lee. The occupational arrangements between young Charles and Archy seemed amiable in the terms of nineteenth-century slavery, and several statements suggest that young Stovall allowed Archy to keep most of his wages.

But the Lee-Stovall relationship was still one of master and slave. In Sacramento Stovall might have felt that relationship threatened by the activities of the free Negro community. He may have heard about the many strikes for freedom made by black men in California. These factors probably contributed to his decision to send Archy back to Mississippi before it was too late, but it is doubtful if Stovall told Archy of his intentions.

Stovall directed Archy to meet him and to board a boat on the Sacramento River, but when Archy arrived he found not Stovall but only a man described as an agent of Stovall. It is clear that Stovall's absence at this moment of departure was crucial to Archy's decision-making process. His master's delay gave the young black man the pause necessary for other considerations to come into play. Archy had been living for several months in close proximity to a community of free and freedom-loving Negroes. They undoubtedly suggested a new and attractive way of life to him. They also must have led him to believe that they could be of aid should he make a strike for freedom.

There was a second consideration. Archy Lee had a potentially serious enemy in Mississippi. He had wounded a white man named Smiley and, while the wound was superficial, the act of resistance in itself in a slave society would forever mark him as a dangerous man. Smiley would never forget the injury; if Archy were to return to Mississippi, he would always have to fear the revenge of the white man.

The fear of Smiley and the real prospect of freedom in California combined in that lonely moment in the boat to propel Archy Lee on his subsequent course of action.

Some facts were revealed about Archy Lee's family sixty years after the court case. In 1918 a letter appeared in the *Journal of Negro History* from a Mrs. Hunt of Marshall, Texas, who identified herself as Archy Lee's niece. From this we learn that Archy, his two brothers, sister and mother were the property of Simeon Stovall, father of Charles Stovall. We also know that young Stovall returned to Mississippi while

Archy did not. The Lee family never heard again about their California-bound member until Mrs. Hunt, the daughter of Archy's only sister, noted reference to Archy in an article in the *Journal of Negro History*.

The Archy Lee case was the cause of a challenge to a duel which was canceled at the last minute. Kentucky-born United States Commissioner George Pen Johnston bore a painful burden as the central legal figure in the last act of Archy's fight for freedom and as a political colleague of those who wanted slave ownership protected. In the days that followed his decision he may have had to endure many derogatory comments, but it was at the Apollo Hall on Pacific Street that anger broke out into the open. From the press one cannot be sure who was the first offender, but Commissioner Johnston and a prominent proslavery Democratic politician named S. H. Brooks (who later joined the Confederate Army) came to a sharp break in their exchanges over the Archy Lee decision. A duel was arranged which was somehow averted just before the principals met at the field.

If Commissioner Johnston was no hero with his political associates, at least he has been celebrated in song and verse, for he provided some of the inspiration for Negro poetry. His name, with others, is mentioned in a hymn written for an Archy Lee victory meeting:

> Sound the glad tidings o'er land and o'er sea
> Our people have triumphed and Archy is free!
> Sing! for the pride of the tyrants is broken:
> The decision of Barnett and Terry reversed.

How vain was their boasting—their plans so long broken;
Archy's free—and Stovall is brought to the dust,
Praise to the judges and praise to the lawyers!
Freedom was their object, and that they obtained.
Stovall was shown it was time to be moving:
He left on the steamer, to lay deeper plans.
But there was a Baker, a Crosby and Tompkins
Before Pen Johnston and did plead for the man [sic].

Even more fittingly, only the major figures are remembered in another victory hymn:

The Year of Archy Lee

Blow ye the trumpet! Blow!
The gladly solemn sound,
Let all the nations know,
To earth's remotest bound.
The year of ARCHY LEE is come:
Return, ye ransomed Stovall, home.

Exalt the Lamb of God:
The sin-atoning Lamb.
Redemption by his blood,
Through all the land proclaim.
The year of ARCHY LEE is come:
Return, ye ransomed Stovall, home.

Ye slaves of sin and hell,
Your liberty receive;
And in Jesus dwell.
And blest in Jesus live.
The year of ARCHY LEE is come:
Return, ye ransomed Stovall, home.

The gospel trumpet hear—
   The news of pardoning grace:
Ye happy souls draw near;
   Behold your Saviour's face.
The year of ARCHY LEE is come:
Return, ye ransomed Stovall, home.

Since its founding in 1974, Heyday Books has occupied a unique niche in the publishing world, specializing in books that foster an understanding of the history, literature, art, environment, social issues, and culture of California and the West. We are a 501(c)(3) nonprofit organization based in Berkeley, California, serving a wide range of people and audiences.

We are grateful for the generous funding we've received for our publications and programs during the past year from foundations and more than three hundred individual donors. Major supporters include:

Anonymous; Audubon California; Judy Avery; Barnes & Noble bookstores; BayTree Fund; B.C.W. Trust III; S. D. Bechtel, Jr. Foundation; Fred & Jean Berensmeier; Book Club of California; Butler Koshland Fund; California State Coastal Conservancy; California State Library; Candelaria Fund; Columbia Foundation; Community Futures Collective; Compton Foundation, Inc.; Malcolm Cravens Foundation; Federated Indians of Graton Rancheria; Fleishhacker Foundation; Wallace Alexander Gerbode Foundation; Richard & Rhoda Goldman Fund; Marion E. Greene; Evelyn & Walter Haas, Jr. Fund: Walter & Elise Haas Fund; James Irvine Foundation; George Frederick Jewett Foundation; Marty & Pamela Krasney; Guy Lampard & Suzanne Badenhoop; LEF Foundation; Dolores Zohrab Liebmann Fund; Michael McCone; National Endowment for the Arts; National Park Service; Philanthropic Ventures Foundation; Alan Rosenus; San Francisco Foundation; William Saroyan Foundation: Seaver Institute; Sandy Cold Shapero; Skirball Foundation; Stanford University; Orin Starn; Swinerton Family Fund; Thendara Foundation; Tom White; and Harold & Alma White Memorial Fund.

For more information about Heyday Institute, our publications and programs, please visit our website at www.heydaybooks.com.

OTHER BAYTREE BOOKS

BayTree Books, a project of Heyday Institute, gives voice to a full range of California experience and personal stories.

Walking Tractor: And Other Country Tales (2008)
Bruce Patterson

Where Light Takes Its Color from the Sea: A California Notebook (2008)
James D. Houston

Tree Barking: A Memoir (2008)
Nesta Rovina

Ticket to Exile (2007)
Adam David Miller

Fast Cars and Frybread: Reports from the Rez (2007)
Gordon Johnson

The Oracles: My Filipino Grandparents in America (2006)
Pati Navalta Poblete

ABOUT THE AUTHOR

Rudolph M. Lapp (1915–2007) received his Ph.D. in U.S. Southern History from the University of California, Berkeley. A professor of history at the College of San Mateo in California for many years, he authored *Blacks in Gold Rush California*, which was given the 1979 California Historical Society Award of Merit and was nominated in 1977 for a Pulitzer Prize.